The
Secret
of the
Spring

**Garry
Leeson**

© 2021 Garry Leeson

All rights reserved. No part of this book may be reproduced or transmitted in any form or by any means, electronic or mechanical, including photocopying, or by any information storage or retrieval system, without permission in writing from the publisher.

Cover design: Rebekah Wetmore
       The inset image is a detail from "The Shoeing" by Sir Edwin Landseer, 1844
Author portrait: Zoe D'Amato
Editor: Andrew Wetmore

ISBN: 978-1-990187-02-5
First edition October, 2021

397 Parker Mountain Road
Granville Ferry NS
B0S 1A0
moosehousepress.com
info@moosehousepress.com

We live and work in Mi'kma'ki, the ancestral and unceded territory of the Mi'kmaq People. This territory is covered by the "Treaties of Peace and Friendship" which Mi'kmaq and Wolastoqiyik (Maliseet) People first signed with the British Crown in 1725. The treaties did not deal with surrender of lands and resources but in fact recognized Mi'kmaq and Wolastoqiyik (Maliseet) title and established the rules for what was to be an ongoing relationship between nations. We are all Treaty people.

For
Beatrix, Henry, Maiella, Isabella, Cooper and Carter,
and, of course,
Andrea

This is a work of fiction, set in a very real place and time. The author has created the characters, conversations, interactions, and events, and any resemblance of any character to any real person is coincidental, with the exception of appearances by certain historical personages. See "On alternate historical fiction" on page 299.

There's an artesian spring on the mountain
That flows efficacious and pure
Where people have come for eons
In search of its magical cure

                                                GHLL

Contents

1: Ham-fisted..9
2: Pretty, blonde daughter............................18
3: A warren of halls.....................................23
4: The dripping girl......................................27
5: Why the tears?...37
6: Will that be all, sir?.................................43
7: A muffled explosive sound......................53
8: Still on the hook......................................61
9: The smithy's horse..................................63
10: What would people say?........................71
11: What terrible sinners we are..................77
12: Enough is enough..................................84
13: The unlikely couple...............................89
14: Pleading eyes...94
15: Not my London.....................................96
16: The clang of a hammer........................102
17: Who could teach me the most.............108
18: Don't you dare stop there!...................114
19: Just trying to hide................................117
20: Half a league onward..........................125
21: Rough shod...127
22: To do whatever he had to....................129
23: Smitten..137
24: The ever-present atlas.........................139
25: You like to leave me hanging..............143
26: The Punch Bowl..................................146
27: Close, but just not right.......................150
28: It can cure things.................................155
29: No life for a woman............................160
30: Your migrating bird.............................162
31: No end of soft moss............................169
32: Something stirred................................171
33: No time for niceties.............................177
34: A note of whimsy................................183

35: Primum non nocere	185
36: Paid in Full	190
37: A hard man	193
38: Made his toes curl	202
39: The world is not as it was	207
40: Gag a maggot	216
41: It is all I have	223
42: But lips were sealed	232
43: Journey into darkness	236
44: What's a contingency?	243
45: There is a thing	247
46: Bash, bash	253
47: In slow time: move out!	259
48: You make of it what you will	265
49: You look a treat	271
50: No parade	278
51: Pretty far-fetched	283
52: Shades of Russia	287
53: Today, Mabel had been lucky	292
On alternate historical fiction	299
Acknowledgements	301
About the author	303
Book club discussion guide	305

1: Ham-fisted

May, 1889

As the sun was slowly making its appearance in the eastern sky, four teams of tired horses stood heads hanging and unattended under a huge elm that shaded the blacksmith shop. It was a small grey-shingled box-like building with a second storey loft under a high-pitched roof. It sat almost on the road next to a large house with an attached woodshed. The weather-worn but neatly kept complex of buildings was located at an intersection where a narrow rutted road came down to meet the main thoroughfare at the base of the North Mountain.

A man driving a fifth team was just arriving at the site. He had manoeuvred his way slowly down that muddy track and after quickly tying his horses to a hitching rail, he rushed inside.

Edgar Leonard, a beefy, ham-fisted bully of a man who liked to be first in line for everything, was not happy as he joined the five men already there waiting for their horses to be shod. He could get away with shoving his way to the head of the line at other locations but he knew better than to try it here. The blacksmith wouldn't put up with that sort of thing in his shop. Edgar had crossed the man only once before at a local fair and barely lived to regret it.

The smithy, Ben Johnson, was a quiet gentle giant of a man. Well over six feet tall, his hair graying, at age fifty-three he was still trim and muscular. When not stooping over the forge or the anvil, he held himself erect with a bearing that spoke of years spent in the military. In fact, he had only taken over the shop eight years earlier after he had indeed retired and mustered out of his cavalry unit at Camp Aldershot further up the Valley.

The inevitable gossip had already begun as the men stood in a circle around Ben watching him work, their faces illuminated by the glowing forge. The men carried the conversation, the smithy only adding occasional comments whenever his exertions on the anvil allowed.

Edgar Leonard, although normally pushy, rude and bellicose, chose this day to stand well back from the rest, still brooding and seething about a situation back home that led to his late arrival and embarrassing wait at the end of the line.

It was only when the bellows occasionally caused the fire to burn brighter that his face was visible at all.

The main topic of conversation, as it had been over the last few years, was the hotel that had been built at the base of the mountain. There was always something new and exciting happening around the place—lots to talk about. The hotel was located on a road parallel to the main route through the Valley

The Secret of the Spring

just a few miles northeast of the town of Middleton. It was a huge pretentious structure whose grandeur was quite out of place amidst the dull-shingled saltbox houses around it.

"It sticks out like a sore thumb," one of the farmers contributed, but he had to admit he sure appreciated the extra money he had earned using his oxen to haul rocks down off the mountain for its foundations.

Another man who was hired to bring guests from the train station in a newly acquired coach financed by the hotel added that since the place had opened for business he had never had it so good.

Old Abe Mosher, holding up a pair of arthritic claws, piped up, "What the hell is so special about that goddamn water that people are coming from all over the world to slurp it up and slosh around in it? I've been watering my horse at that spring on the way to town for years, drunk lots it myself and just look at me and that spavined old bastard in the corner who calls himself a horse!"

The smithy, who had just finished turning the heel on a red hot shoe and was cooling it in a pail of water, wiped his brow and spoke over the sizzle. "You've got to admit the place is creating a lot of jobs, and I hear now they're desperate to find girls to work as maids in the place."

"Maybe they'll take my old woman!" Abe chimed in again.

"They ain't that desperate," someone said and they all laughed and shook their heads in agreement.

When the laughter died down, Murray Daniels, a lanky middle-aged farmer who had made the long trek from his place on South Mountain, stepped forward, swept off his straw hat and inserted himself into the conversation.

"I ain't seen any of you boys since I was in here last and that was quite a while ago. I guess Ben here is doing too good a job of tacking my team's shoes on. They seem to stay put a lot longer than the ones old Percy used to hammer away at."

"Easy now," Ben said. "Percy Smith was a good blacksmith—he was just getting a little old for the job."

"Yeah, I guess you're right," Murray said. "The old bugger complained that his muscles were getting wormy for years before he got that kick that finally laid him up for good."

Then, fixing a glance at a man standing close to a soot smeared window, he inquired, "That was one of your horses, wasn't it, Jeff?"

"No damned way!" a voice shot back. "It was a logging company horse. Not my responsibility. He was a mean, dangerous son of a bitch but the best damned yard horse in Nova Scotia."

"Anyway," Murray continued, "I'm glad to see you boys. The only time I get to have a jaw or a visit with anybody is over here or in that old church up on the mountain. And by the way, did you fellas hear about the kerfuffle that went on up our way a while ago?"

When no one responded, he continued, "You fellas might have heard tell of the Bentley brothers. They

The Secret of the Spring

farm together up by me and work in the woods when they get the chance. For years the boys have been taking turns, one staying at the logging camp a few miles south of them overnight while the other hikes home to do the chores. Bob, the older brother, has been married to his wife, Gloria, for about ten years now and they have about that number of children to show for it. Jim, the younger brother, who is part owner of the farm, has always stayed with them.

"Well, it seemed like a good arrangement—been going on for years—but then, last month, things took a turn for the worse. Bob decided to make a visit back home on one of the nights that he was to stay at the camp. Bob's new heifer was due to calve and he was worried about her. He was pleased when he found his new calf waiting in the barn, but not so pleased when he headed into the house and found his wife and his brother together in his bed. Turns out they'd been going at it for years! All the shouting, bashing and bruising caused their neighbour, old Mrs. Adcock, to come a-running, and by morning the mountain was buzzing like a beehive. The following Sunday Deacon Jones had the pair of sinners in front of the congregation confessing while he tore a strip off them and called for the wrath of God to descend upon them and the whole congregation to shun them.

"Bob wasn't in attendance. He had tried to return Gloria to her family, but when they arrived at her old home, her father told his daughter to stay in Bob's buggy, saying that he figured Bob must have known

Gloria was damaged goods when he hooked up with her.

"The shunning hasn't taken hold because Jim slipped away and headed to the States and Gloria being the only one in the parish who can play the organ —well, what can you do?

"So now Bob and Gloria are back in the house together and things seem to be settling down. All that's left is a lot of speculating around the quilting circle concerning which of the brothers might have sired which of Gloria's brood."

At that Abe leapt back into the conversation. "By God, I knowed that Gloria, and that might be quite a puzzle for those quilters to unwind. She used to come down and pick apples with us. She was a good worker and full of fun, but as some of you fellas might know, aside from what might have been going on at home, Gloria was inclined to stray further afield once in a while. There may be more variety in that little herd of hers than anybody will ever know."

Ben halted his hammer's swing down to the anvil mid-stroke, cocked his eyebrow and shot a look of mock admonition in the old man's direction.

Unruffled, Abe slumped forward, retrieved the jug he had been holding protectively between his feet, balanced it on his shoulder and took a long swig.

"I thought you was never going to haul that thing out, Abe," one of the men said as he positioned himself for the second swig.

The jug made its way around a few times to all present, including Edgar Leonard, who temporarily

The Secret of the Spring

stopped sulking so that he could participate in his favourite indulgence. Only the smithy, who never touched the stuff, declined.

It was inevitable that several of the men would not be making the trip home completely sober, but usually, even if a man had so much to drink that he couldn't hold onto the reins, the others would lift him into his wagon and his horses would find their own way home.

When Edgar Leonard finally had his horses shod at the end of the day, he wasn't really drunk – he'd had just enough of Abe's smuggled rum to fuel the fire that had been burning in the back of his mind all day. He was mad as hell and he had good reason.

When he was safely out of earshot Edgar began to mumble to himself. *Those lazy goddamned boys of mine—not one of them was out of bed when I left this morning. If I'd had a little help getting the team harnessed, I might not have got here so late and wasted my whole day. I'll bet the bastards are still in bed and the cows not milked—three boys and not a useful one in the batch.*

Edgar's one calming thought was that his daughter, Lilly, would have his dinner waiting for him. Lilly, a pretty little fifteen-year-old with white-blonde hair, was unlike her brothers in all respects. She had taken on all the chores around the house after her mother died, without a word of complaint.

The trip back up the mountain took longer than usual. Edgar didn't want to hurry the horses—they might injure themselves while they were getting used to the new sharp-caulked shoes Ben had shod them with. But the longer he took, the angrier he got.

"By god, those boys better have the chores done!" he told the horses.

When Edgar finally arrived in the dooryard, he reined in the horses and climbed off the wagon, whip in hand.

One of those lazy buggers is gonna put these horses into the barn, he thought, testing the whip. *And I hope he tries to get out of it.*

As his foot hit the first creaking board on the porch stairs he heard them: first a scream, then a whimper, followed by the boys' voices.

"Hold her down!" one said.

"Hold her down yourself, you was first last time!'

"Was not! Gordie was!"

The voices ceased at the sound of Edgar's boots thundering up the stairs.

By the time he reached the second floor bedroom, the youngest of the boys was already out the window and sliding off the porch roof. Edgar set about the remaining brothers with his whip, slashing mercilessly at them.

When they attempted to get by him and escape, he used his fists and his hobnailed boots over and over again. The boys screamed and begged him to stop but he kept on until he finally exhausted himself and slumped down on the foot of the bed.

Seeing that it was safe to escape their father's wrath, the boys snuck out of the room, one crawling on all fours and the other staggering while covering an empty eye socket with the back of a bloody hand.

Edgar, still breathing heavily, turned his head toward his daughter. She was curled up against the iron headboard with her knees bent up and her arms hugging her legs tightly against her naked breast. When he had recovered enough to stand, he tossed the old quilt from the chair over the sobbing girl and, without a word, headed downstairs.

2: Pretty, blonde daughter

Two days had passed since the incident and Edgar had spent most of his time sitting at the kitchen table, drinking and trying to figure out what to do. In some respects things were back to normal: the girl was going about her chores as if nothing had happened and two of the boys had slunk home and were making a big show of the few chores they were doing, trying to get back on his good side.

The third boy had run to the neighbour's after he lost his eye to the whip and they had taken him into town to the doctor, who cleaned the remains of the eye out and sewed the lid down.

They'll probably have the law on me. He tipped the now empty jug of rum up, hoping to find a last drop. He was trying to figure out where he had gone wrong and what he was going to do about it. It just wasn't fair—he seemed to have all the bad luck.

Maybe he should have listened to his father when he warned him that he shouldn't marry a girl who was probably his first cousin but he wasn't sure she was, so he went ahead and did it anyway. The minister didn't object.

It was only a lot later, after his father died and he

heard stories about the old man's sleeping around, that he realized that Lisa, his wife, might have been even more closely related. That would account for those drooling nitwit sons he had sired.

He should have been proud of his pretty, blonde daughter, but he had his suspicions about the discounts a travelling salesman had been giving his wife the year before Lilly was born. It didn't sit right with him. The good thing was that he wasn't singled out or made a fool of because there was quite a crop of blond babies on the mountain that year.

He gave the woman a good hiding anyway, maybe too good because she was never quite right after that. Then she upped and died a couple of years ago, leaving him to take care of everything.

He'd been through all that and now, when life should've been a lot easier for him, he found himself saddled with three useless boys who had started pestering Lilly. He ought to have seen it coming; she had matured early and there were few girls on the mountain as pretty and well-built as she was. He had to admit he'd had a few weak moments himself and maybe sat her on his knee too often when he was drunk.

He didn't ask the girl how long it had been going on with the boys—he didn't really want to know. What he did know was that it had to stop and stop now.

He was pretty sure he was going to get a visit from the law concerning his son's eye 'accident' and he didn't want them snooping around only to find out what had been going on up in that bedroom. He had to get the girl away from the farm and the sooner the better.

He was still weighing the few options he had when the kitchen door opened a crack and a bruised face peered in and said, "Pa, one of those new shoes has come off Dolly."

As he thought about returning to the blacksmith's shop, the conversation of his last visit came back to him. Remembering the smith's comment about the hotel needing maids, he called out, "Lilly, get cleaned up. We're going down to the Valley."

Lilly wondered what her father wanted, but she didn't often get the chance to go anywhere. So she took the stairs two at a time and headed for her closet, where she kept one of her mother's old dresses. It was the best she had, and when she'd worn the frock before, her father said that she filled it out a lot better than her mother had. The faded blue gingham dress was a bit tight and had had more than a few repairs over the years, but it was still Lilly's treasure.

After slipping it on, she ran a comb through her hair, added a pink ribbon and checked herself in the cracked mirror on her dresser. She figured she didn't look too bad—as long as nobody noticed the hand-me-down boots she was wearing.

Her brothers had hustled around getting the team hitched and by the time she'd finished primping and made her way to the front porch, her father was already waiting in the wagon. One of her brothers made a move to help her up, but one look from his father had him backing away warily.

Edgar let the horses take their time on the way down the sloping road—he didn't want the mare with the unshod foot to damage it further before he got to the smithy and, anyway, he needed time to think.

Lilly was glad that her father wasn't questioning her about what had happened. She couldn't have told him much because, really, she hadn't been there. He wouldn't have understood that, when it had started, she had found a place in her mind where she could hide and avoid the pain and terror. She had been in that special place of safety when her father had found her with the boys. It had taken her longer to leave it on that occasion because it had also become somewhere to hide from her father. There was no point telling him that he wouldn't understand—she didn't understand it herself.

He only spoke his first words to her just as the blacksmith shop came into view. "I've got some things to talk over with Ben. You just sit there and keep your trap shut!"

Ben had heard the team approaching and was waiting outside the shop when Edgar swung into the yard. He didn't need to be told what the problem was. He went right over and picked up Molly's leg and examined the hoof.

"It doesn't look too bad." Then, noticing the shoe in Edgar's hand, he said, "Don't bother to unhitch her. I'll reset the shoe where she is."

A couple of licks with the rasp and a few well-placed nails and the job was done.

"What do I owe you?" Edgar asked, knowing full well that Ben guaranteed his work and wouldn't be charging him anything. A wave of Ben's hand ended the transaction and Edgar changed the subject.

"By the way," he said, trying to sound casual, "the other day you mentioned that the new hotel was looking for maids. When I told Lilly here about it, she got all excited and wanted me to bring her down to see if they would hire her. Do you know who's in charge over there?"

Ben looked up at Lilly, who looked confused. "I look after the hotel manager's saddle horse. He's the fellow that mentioned it, so you should talk to him. Name's Worthington."

"I thank you for that," Edgar said, climbing up on the wagon.

"I would use the back door."

As the pair drove off, Ben had a good long look at Lilly. He knew that, considering the manager's reputation with the ladies, she wouldn't have any trouble getting the job.

3: A warren of halls

It was only a quick trot over to the hotel. Edgar hadn't been by the spa since it opened—he always used a different route when heading into Middleton. When he saw the crowds of well-dressed patrons and their fancy carriages at the front of the hotel, he felt sorely out of place but pressed on anyway.

He found the lane to the rear of the main building, made a wide sweep and turned in. He had just stopped the horses and was preparing to climb out of the wagon box when a little bald man, dressed neatly in a black jacket with a white shirt and crisply starched collar, came running toward him, shouting.

"See here! See here! You can't leave that vehicle there."

"I've come to see Mr. Worthington," Edgar said.

"Do you have an appointment?" The little man scrutinized the wagon disdainfully

"I ain't got no appointment but I got my daughter here and Ben Johnson said you was looking for maids."

"It seems you have been misinformed, so would you kindly remove this heap of a wagon before any of our guests see it?"

Edgar turned red in the face and started fingering his buggy whip, judging the distance between him and the cocky little man.

Just then a window opened on the first floor of the hotel and a handsome, grey-haired man in his forties leaned out.

"What's going on out there?" he called out.

"Just a little misunderstanding, Mr. Worthington, but I've handled it."

"Well, for God's sake, send them on their way. I've got enough to trouble me already."

"You heard him, off you go!" the little man said with finality in his voice.

Suppressing the urge to give the fellow a farewell cut with his whip, Edgar leaned forward to take up the reins. As he did, Lilly, who had previously been blocked from the view of the man in the window, became visible.

The atmosphere immediately changed. "Hold on a minute, James," Worthington said. "No need to be rude. Bring the gentleman up to my office."

Handing the reins over to Lilly, Edgar climbed down from the wagon and followed the man in the back door of the hotel, through a warren of halls that smelled of fresh paint, and finally across the lobby of the hotel into a large office.

"Have a seat," Worthington said to Edgar, pointing to one of the wooden chairs in lieu of an upholstered one that he judged might have to be scrapped after an encounter with Edgar's smelly trousers. "Now, what can I do for you, my good man?"

The Secret of the Spring

"Ben Johnson says you's looking for girls to work here."

"Ben seems to be a good fellow so I guess, on his recommendation, we might consider it. Tell me about her."

"Well, sir, Lilly's fifteen years old. She's a hard worker and can do most any chores—took over all the cooking and cleaning when her mother died. Don't eat a whole lot and don't sass back."

The negotiations went quickly after that. There was only one hesitation, when Edgar said he'd be picking up the girl's pay himself. At first Worthington was not comfortable with that arrangement, but after getting to his feet and walking, hands clasped behind his back, to the window where he could see the girl again, he turned back to Edgar and agreed. What did he care what happened to the girl's meagre monthly pittance?

"Done, then," Edgar said. "She can start the now."

"Now? Right now?"

"I don't want to have to haul her down the mountain a second time."

Worthington hesitated. Whenever he had to deal with the locals he felt like he was peering into an unfamiliar world with very odd customs. Finally he said, "All right, then. You can bring her things along the next time you come this way."

What things? Edgar thought to himself.

James, the man who had met them in the yard, led him back down to where Lilly waited in the wagon. After Edgar's terse, "Get down and go with him, girl,"

Lilly slipped down using the spokes of the wheel as a ladder.

She followed James toward the rear door of the hotel, glancing back quickly in her father's direction for some sign of reassurance. But he had already taken up his whip and was turning the horses toward the road.

4: The dripping girl

Worthington watched from his window as Edgar drove away and then, catching James' attention, signalled for him to collect the girl and bring her to his office. He stepped away from the window, turned to the mirror he kept mounted on his office wall and began smoothing his moustache and straightening his hair. *Too many grey hairs these days—time to dig out the bottle of black henna again.*

The arrival of this girl was a delightful distraction for the harried man. He liked what he had glimpsed of her as she sat in her father's wagon, but distances can be deceiving. He wanted, needed, a closer look.

He heard the sound of approaching footsteps but, lost in his thoughts, continued staring into the mirror and primping until a vision of her standing framed in the doorway behind him appeared beside his reflection. He studied her this way for several seconds before he regained his composure enough to turn and greet her.

There was something about her, even packaged as she was in her tattered clothes. She displayed a simple, unblemished beauty. He moved closer to where she stood, nervously staring at the floor. He wanted to touch her—he needed to touch her.

Standing close to her, he detected the odour of lye soap masking a faint but pungent musk of wood smoke and farm kitchen. He didn't find it unpleasant. On the contrary, it seemed exotic and strangely stimulating.

Steadying a trembling hand he reached forward and lifted her chin up toward him to get a better look.

"Open your eyes, Lilly. That's your name, isn't it? Let's see those pretty eyes of yours. No? Oh, well, no hurry. We'll get better acquainted later. You go with James now."

He continued to stare in her direction as she turned to follow James out the door. "You do speak, don't you, Lilly?"

"Yes, sir," came a faint reply.

"Good, good. Now off you go. "

As she moved out of sight he scurried forward and craned his neck around the door jamb for a final look.

Her flimsy dress clung to and exposed the delightful contours of her body, leaving little need for speculation about what wonders were hiding beneath.

Worthington was smitten. He didn't really want another involvement—what with his ongoing liaisons with several of the younger maids below stairs and the obligatory attention he was often required to give to overstimulated female imbibers of the cure, his dance card, as it were, was already quite full.

Business had been good, too good. The hotel

The Secret of the Spring

could accommodate one hundred guests and, in the right season, the rooms were always full. His list of regulars included some very important people and in the short time the spa had been open, the hotel register had begun to look like a who's who of royalty and the rich and famous.

Recently he had been forced to turn down several requests for reservations at the spa and that posed a problem. The hotel's owner, Captain Hall, had already reprimanded him for slighting, as he put it, 'a very important member of British aristocracy.'

Now an equally important letter with a broken red wax seal was resting to one side of his desk. Its priority meant he was once again going to have to disappoint someone, and he wasn't prepared to make the decision on his own. He scribbled a quick note requesting a meeting with Captain Hall.

~

"And what have we here, sir?" Mrs. Stronach said as James shoved Lilly through the open door of the little room that served as the Housekeeper's office.

"Another of Mr. Worthington's projects," he said. "Do what you can with her—I think a good bath might be the first order of business."

"Come in and sit down, my dear. This is a surprise. I didn't realize we were still hiring, but good to see you all the same. Many hands make light work!"

Mrs. Stronach could see that the girl was anxious and wary of the situation she was finding herself in so she rose from her own seat behind her desk and stepped forward to gently guide Lilly into one of the two chairs designated for visitors. She pulled the other chair around to face Lilly and then sat down, taking Lilly's hands in her own two.

Speaking softly, she said, "Now, no need to be afraid, dear. It's all new and different but you'll soon get used to it. Are you hungry? Can I get you something to eat or drink? Maybe some tea? What about a nice hot cup of tea?"

When there was no response she decided to start over. "How rude of me. I haven't even introduced myself. My name is Mrs. Stronach, but everybody at the hotel calls me Matron. What do people call you, my dear?"

"My name is Lilly Leonard," she whispered.

"What a lovely name. I'll tell you a little secret. Nobody around here knows it, but my first name is Lilly also—well, actually, it's Lillian but everybody called me Lilly when I was your age. How old are you, Lilly?"

"I'm fifteen, Mrs., Mrs...."

"Try 'Matron', Lilly, it's easier to remember."

"I'm fifteen this year, Matron."

"I'll tell you what, Lilly, if I can't talk you into something to eat or drink, why don't we two flowers take a stroll down to where we can get you started on your new job?"

Mrs. Stronach took Lilly by the arm and led her down a narrow staircase, and along a darkened hall

The Secret of the Spring

toward the rear of the basement. It ended at the entrance to the large steamy laundry room.

In addition to the wooden barrel washtubs, the room contained several bathtubs that had been damaged in transit from England. The chipped porcelain was deemed unsuitable for the guests on the upper floors but a windfall for the staff and the only opportunity for them to sample the spa's healing spring waters. There was a roster that designated which days the male and female employees could use the tubs and, fortunately for Lilly, it was women's day. Only early morning bathing was permitted, so now in the early afternoon, the tubs were unused and available.

The room was occupied by five older women, three of them elbow deep in the wooden washtubs, using their scrub boards, and two others busy twisting the crank handles on large wooden rollers, squeezing the water out of the sodden hotel bed sheets.

"Here's a job for you, Margaret," Mrs. Stronach said to one of the washtub women. "Give her a bath and find her a uniform." Turning to leave she stopped and spoke again. "And burn those smelly boots and that God-forsaken dress she's wearing. Bring her back to me when she is fit for civilized society."

"You're a lucky one, my dear," Margaret hummed again and again as she repeatedly dipped her pail into one of the wash tubs, borrowing enough of the used, soapy, warm water to partially fill a tub for her new charge. "We only get to use cold water when we have our baths in the morning."

Lilly turned shyly toward the wall as Margaret slipped the soiled dress over her head and tossed it aside. The dress was all she'd worn, and now she stood naked, shielding herself with her hands and her arms. Her body appeared perfect, with the flawless ivory skin that the pampered female clients in the rooms above would have died for.

When Margaret pulled out the girl's hair ribbon, the tresses spread over her shoulders and down to the level of her pert breasts. The only feature that belied perfection was the condition of her calloused, work-worn hands—one of which Margaret held and scrutinized as she helped the girl into the tepid, soapy water of the tub. As Lilly lifted her leg over the edge of the tub, Margaret saw the bottom of her foot.

"Dear God! Those hands and feet of yours are going to need some special attention. Doris, bring me that scrub brush!"

Margaret set about the girl's hands and feet with a vengeance, but when it came to her hair she treated it with a mother's gentleness.

"Doris, let's try some of that soap the lady from New York left you last week."

"Nothin' doin'. I'm savin' it for Christmas."

"C'mon, Doris, we only need a bit."

Doris reluctantly came over to help wash Lilly's hair, but she and Margaret were soon joking and splashing each other as they playfully soaped, massaged and rinsed the girl.

The Secret of the Spring

"Close your eyes just one last time, dear. I know it's cold but Doris insisted on getting it right out of the cistern. She says it's best for the hair."

Margaret dumped the final bucket over the shivering girl's head while one of the women who had gathered to watch the fun offered several flannels.

Margaret and Doris helped the dripping girl to her feet as several hands proffered the towelling. A great deal of rubbing and patting ensued before two more women arrived, bearing fresh underwear and a new uniform still warm from ironing.

Lily dressed herself quickly, fumbling at the clasps and hooks under so many watchful eyes. Then Margaret took her hand and walked her back to Mrs. Stronach's office.

With Matron was another girl of about Llly's age, in the same sort of uniform.

"Lilly, I'd like you to meet Angeline," Mrs. Stronach said. "She's around the same age as you so I thought you two might like to share a room together."

The two girls stood side by side in front of the Matron's desk, Lilly, a petite and pretty blonde beside Angeline with her full curvaceous body, shiny black hair and beautiful face.

"Are you content with that arrangement, Lilly?"

Lilly remained silent, not knowing quite how to respond.

"I'll take that as a 'yes', then. Now, what about you, Angeline. Do you think there's room enough up in that little room of yours?"

"Oui, oui, oui! Yes, yes, yes!! C'mon, Lilly, let's go!"

Angeline grabbed Lilly's hand and practically dragged her through the door.

The two girls went hand in hand, with Angeline showing the way, to the third storey room they were to share. They climbed up a steep staircase on the side wall of a huge storeroom at the rear of the hotel. It was constructed with crude steps of raw planks and had no banister.

"There is a much better staircase in the hotel itself," Angeline said, "but it is not for us. We are forbidden. We go this way to our room. Stay near the wall, or you may miss your step and fall."

The tiny room at the top of the stairs had two narrow beds and a wardrobe. There was a large window that looked down over the stable yard and filled the room with sunshine. On the wall beside each bed was a finger lamp mounted on a bracket so the girls could light up the room at the end of the long work days.

To Lilly, the notion that this wonderful room was to be partially hers was like a dream come true. Turning away from Angeline, she used her new apron to wipe away a tear. Angeline left her to her thoughts for several minutes before returning with a huge grey cat in her arms.

"This is Yves," she said as she put him down and retrieved a dish from under her bed. "I give him scraps from the kitchen. Mr. Worthington doesn't like me feeding him. He says I have a job and Yves has a job and his is to catch rats in the storeroom. I don't pay him any mind, though."

The Secret of the Spring

Over the next few days, Angeline, ever helpful and kind, took Lilly in hand, showing her the ins and outs of her job. Lilly wasn't long settling into her new life at the hotel. She was a quick learner and an eager worker. Chores that seemed so demanding to the other women were nothing compared to the drudgery she had endured at home. She still spoke little and only managed the occasional smile, but willingly did anything that was asked of her.

The two girls did all the menial tasks: they scrubbed floors, washed dishes, emptied chamber pots and were at the beck and call of the rest of the staff. They spent a great deal of their time attending to the guests in the bathhouse, hauling hot water to their tubs and preparing mud baths. They snickered quietly to themselves as they watched the overweight women, dressed head to toe in woollen bathing costumes, immerse themselves in the outdoor galvanized tubs and gulp down glass after glass of the bitter-tasting water.

The men's side of the building was more of a challenge for them. The girls had to be quick on their feet to avoid the constant groping of the aging men, who deluded themselves into believing the waters were actually restoring their lost virility.

The days were long and some of the nights even longer. The girls were responsible for cleaning up after the Captain's banquets. These affairs often continued into the wee hours of the morning with the patrons confusing the anaesthetizing effect of the rum provided with the healing quality of the spring waters.

Through a partially open kitchen door Angeline and Lilly enjoyed watching the antics of the spirited guests and took full advantage of the opportunity to snatch morsels of the wonderful food the Captain served. They were quickly becoming fast friends and for the first time ever Lilly was able to relax without worrying about the horrors of her home.

When Lilly discovered she was starting her period a few days later, Angeline was the one who ran downstairs to get some linen rags for her from the laundry room.

5: Why the tears?

Three weeks seemed to fly by for Lilly. She was kept busy from dawn 'til dusk, but a whole new world was opening up to her. People who dressed differently, sounded different and came from places she'd never heard of surrounded her, needed her and thanked her. With minor exceptions, she and Angeline were always together—taking their morning baths or enjoying their few leisure hours in each other's company.

The only time there was any tension between the girls was when Lilly, in an unusually flippant manner, said that she thought that the healing properties of the spa waters were a bunch of nonsense and that the water from her dad's farm on the mountain would do the people just as much good.

Angeline sat up on her bed and frowned. "Lilly, you don't know what you're talking about. Those people downstairs can't buy what this water does. They can't have its magic because it isn't theirs. This spring belongs to everyone—it always has. It has always cured us when we were sick. Building the hotel stopped us all from coming here and made us feel like trespassers."

Lilly cast her eyes down in embarrassment. She

hadn't meant any offence. They were friends—best friends.

Angeline sensed her disquiet and in a calmer voice, explained, "My family still drinks the water and makes mudpacks to cure our wounds but we must come with jugs and bottles at night to take what is rightfully ours. That's how I ended up here. My mother was sick and my father sent me for the waters. I was at the spring in the middle of the night filling my jug when Mr. Worthington found me. He said I was trespassing and gave me a choice: go to jail or stay and work at the hotel."

"But what about your mother?" Lilly asked.

"Mr. Worthington promised he would send a case of the water to my mother, so I figured I'd better stay a while. And he sends my wages to my family."

Lilly nodded her head in an unspoken apology as the girls lay back down. Even though they shared their attic room, there were still some secrets between them.

There was no one Lilly would rather spend time with than Angeline and she'd assumed Angie, as she'd started to call her, felt the same way. When they weren't working together, they were eating together, strolling together, spending almost every hour in each other's company, or so Lilly thought. In fact, on the few occasions when Angie had insisted on going for long walks in the woods up the slope above the hotel by herself, Lilly assumed she just needed some alone time.

But one day when Lilly returned to their room,

The Secret of the Spring

she found Angie sitting on her bed, sobbing, while she combed grass and pine needles out of her hair. She went to comfort her and when she sat down beside her, the girl fell into her arms.

"What's the matter Angie? Why the tears?"

Lilly daubed the stricken girl's face and repeatedly asked what was wrong, but her silence persisted. Eventually they both just sat hugging each other and staring silently out the window.

Finally Angeline rose and opened the window, letting the cool air refresh her. Lilly joined her and the two stared out into the stable yard and the dark forest that stretched beyond it.

After a time they heard the sound of hoof beats approaching, and Mr. Worthington calling out to James as he rode in. He dismounted, handed off the reins, and hurried toward the hotel's rear door.

At the door he glanced up toward their window. His eyes met with Angeline's briefly before she turned away and buried her face in Lilly's chest. Her sobbing intensified and in a muffled voice she said, "Don't ever let that bastard near you!"

~

Worthington carried on into his office and turned to his favourite afternoon tipple: the Captain's black Jamaican rum. It was his one solace in the God-forsaken backwater he now found himself in. Life had not been fair to him. If it hadn't been for the accusations of that damned housekeeper in Torquay, he might still be the manager of The Imperial Hotel.

He had finished the contents of two shot glasses and was contemplating a third when there was a rap on his door.

"Do come in, Mrs. Stronach," he said with a touch of rancour in his voice.

"Sorry to disturb you, sir," she said, stepping up to the front of his desk.

"What is it.?" Annoyance was only thinly veiled in his voice. "I hope everything is shipshape—you know how particular the Captain is."

Mrs. Stronach adjusted her glasses, took a deep breath and blurted out the purpose of her visit "I'm going to need some more ready cash."

Worthington grimaced and shifted further back in his chair as the matron raised her notebook and started to read.

"First, the farmers bringing us eggs don't like waiting a month before they get paid. They tell me that they can easily take their eggs to the general store in town and exchange them for staples straight away. Second, I'm in a similar situation with the women baking bread and making pies and other desserts for us. You know we can't get by without their help. There's no way our kitchen could keep up with the demand, especially at this time of year."

"They will get their pay in good time."

"Mrs. Morse has flatly refused to bring us any more baked beans and brown bread if she can't leave with cash in hand. Some of our clients tell me her beans and bread seem to be as effective on their constitutions as our water so we need to keep her happy."

Worthington shook his head slowly.

"Third, Mr. Hutchison is complaining that there wasn't enough sawdust used in the ice house when it was loaded last winter. The ice is melting fast and he's worried about the milk and butter and the sides of beef hanging in there. And finally, we almost had a mutiny last week when the Captain instructed me to tell the maids that they would have to help plucking chickens for the kitchen."

At that she lowered her list and waited.

"Are you quite finished?"

"I suppose so, for now, sir. But—"

"No more buts, please! These local bandits seem to have us over a barrel, so you shall have the ready cash you need, but..." He shook his head. There was no easy way out.

"First, make the best deal you can over the eggs. I'm sure Mr. Illsley at the general store is not giving his groceries away. As for the baked goods, not all breads, cakes and pies are created equal, so judge them individually and only pay what you must."

"All right."

"The ice house was not filled on my watch. All I can do at this point is pray that we do not have a summer of spoiled meat, sour milk and rancid butter ahead of us. The women in the laundry room are more suited to the chicken plucking task. I'll let you deal with that one."

"Me?"

"Now, if there is nothing more, you can take your leave and I'll arrange for the funds to be taken to your office."

Mrs. Stronach closed her notebook and turned toward the door, but then turned back. "May I ask who exactly this special guest is that we are expecting?"

"No, you may not, madam. However, I will tell you that he and his companions are men of the sea and very important."

Mrs. Stronach drew in her breath and frowned. Their differences in such minor details aside, they were both afraid of the burly Captain, with his dark beard, piercing eyes, and hard hands. Captain Hall ran the hotel like a ship.

Mrs. Stronach would have preferred he'd run it like a hotel. In particular, she hated all the nautical references that he had recently insisted that the staff use: floors called decks, the front desk a fo'c'sle, the kitchen a galley, and now, a final insult, her own office a hold. What had started as a ploy by the Captain to amuse the visiting shipping magnate Samuel Cunard had become her personal ongoing torment. He had even taken to piping certain guests aboard as they climbed the steps to the front veranda.

And now, dear God! she thought as she turned to leave, *more of this naval nonsense.*

6: Will that be all, sir?

The following day the Flying Bluenose Express train pulled into Middleton station and four men in British Royal Navy uniforms disembarked. The three older men busied themselves removing suitcases and fishing gear from a private compartment while the fourth, a man in his early twenties, stood ramrod straight in his officer's uniform, hands behind his back, supervising. He was around six feet tall, with dark hair, a well-trimmed, fashionable beard and the ruddy complexion that spoke of time spent on the open sea.

Their luggage retrieved, the three older sailors hovered protectively around the officer until the hotel's horse-drawn van pulled up to the station platform. They took the three-mile trip to the hotel at a constant trot, and when they arrived, a puffed up Captain Hall, standing at attention on the veranda, greeted them. The young officer, accompanied by a sailor on either side, offered Hall only a cursory nod as he entered the hotel.

Once in the lobby, one of the older men mistook Worthington for a bellhop and thrust the luggage toward him. "Don't just stand there gawking, skipper. Grab them cases and lead on!"

"What! I'm not…I'm not…James, where is James?" *Useless bugger is never around when you need him.*

"Hop to it now!" the old sailor barked as he swung his own kit bag onto his shoulder and glanced down at the two large leather valises.

James, who was hidden from the manager's view behind a crowd of curious employees in the entrance to the dining room, stayed put and chuckled to himself as he watched Worthington struggle up the main stairway, lugging the heavy baggage.

Humbled and embarrassed, the Captain escorted the remaining sailor over to the desk and watched while he went through the formalities. When the sailor finished, the Captain stole a look at the register. None of the names inscribed were familiar.

A short time later the young officer summoned the Captain to his suite of rooms.

"See here, Captain Hall, I must apologize for ignoring you when I arrived. But, damn it, man, the arrangement was that I was to be here incognito. Any fuss at my arrival might have given the game away!"

"Aye, aye, Your Highness. It won't happen again," the Captain said, standing stiffly with his cap in his hand. "If there's anything I can do to make your stay more enjoyable here, just let me know. Please, Sire—your wish is my command."

"For God's sake, stop spouting all that nonsense and stop calling me 'Your Highness.' Now leave me be."

The Captain, dejected, bowed and left the room.

The following morning the four seamen took a very early breakfast in their rooms, then set off in a four-seater buggy provided by the hotel for the lake and a day's fishing. They had been given a well-provisioned picnic basket to see them through the day, but when they arrived back just as the sun was setting, they were famished. One of the fellows took three strings of fat trout down to the kitchen for immediate preparation.

The chef, an aging Philippine whom the Captain had picked up during one of his voyages years ago, wasn't happy about having to fire up the stoves again. They had prepared and served all the main meals already, but he complied, smiling as he addressed the authoritative old sailor with a string of Spanish curses made to sound like compliments. The sailor just smiled back and left none the wiser.

The next morning Captain Hall hit the deck early. His little cook had complained to him and he wanted to caution the rest of the staff that they were to be instantly at the sailors' disposal, no matter what was required of them. He conducted the short meeting in the kitchen and then sent the twenty-five or so women and handful of men about their business.

As he started to head back upstairs, an older chambermaid stopped him in his path.

"What is it, woman?"

She paused uncomfortably. "I was sent to the young officer's room, Captain Sir, but he doesn't seem to want me, sir. The young man wishes to speak with you immediately."

Turning quickly on her heels, instead of returning the way she had come, she headed to Mrs. Stronach's room with a hurt look on her face.

Whatever now? the Captain thought as he straightened his tie and headed up the stairs.

Checking his tie yet again, he knocked. Hearing a cheery, "Enter!" he cautiously made his way in and closed the door behind him.

The young officer, in a silk dressing gown, was standing by an open window, cigarette in hand. He flipped open a silver case and offered one to the Captain, who declined. "I'm more of a cigar man, Your – sir." He immediately regretted his refusal.

"Pity. I don't seem to have any with me, but I'll remember for next time. I wanted to speak to you about a matter of some delicacy. I'm hoping we can discuss it in complete confidence. Sailor to sailor, as it were."

The Captain nodded agreement. The mood between them had obviously lifted and the young man continued, "It's about the chambermaid you have provided. She seems to be very attentive and thorough..."

His eyes met with the Captain's and authority was re-established. "But see here, if I wanted to be wakened in the morning by a long hairy face, I should choose to sleep in your stables!"

He chuckled at his little joke and continued, "We're both men of the world, Captain, and I am sure

The Secret of the Spring

that you know what it's like to spend months at sea with only men to look at. In the short time you've got ashore you want pretty female faces around you—some memories to take back to sea."

"Certainly, sir, but she is the most experienced maid we have. She has served some of the most important men on the continent."

The young officer paused, ashed his cigarette, looked the Captain straight in the eyes and said, "I'll be plain, Captain. I mean to have someone else. I've noticed a young blonde girl attending to your other guests and I wish her to be assigned to my room."

"But that girl has only been with us for three weeks and has very little experience."

"And I shall make allowances for that," the young officer said with finality in his voice.

Mrs. Stronach called Lilly to her office and explained what had occurred and what she was now required to do.

For the first time since her arrival, Lilly showed true emotion. "Oh please, don't make me do it, Mrs. Stronach! I can't do it, I know I can't. I don't know how. I don't know how to fold the bed properly; I've never managed a full room on my own before. I'll just botch it up and embarrass everyone, I don't have any—"

"Stop at once, you silly girl. You will do it and that's that. I shall help you prepare. The sailors are off fishing again and you and I are going to spend the day getting you ready. By the time they return you

47

will know enough tricks of the trade to get by, I assure you."

So while the other maids watched, snickered and pretended not to be offended, Mrs. Stronach spent several hours showing Lilly the ropes, as the Captain would have termed it. By the time the fishermen returned, the young officer's room was perfectly laid out.

Lilly's last job for the evening would be a brief appearance in the room to turn his bed down. She knocked tentatively on the door. Hearing no response, let herself in.

"And who would you be?" the young officer said, pretending to be surprised by her presence.

"Lilly, my name is Lilly, sir." She tried the short curtsy she had learned earlier that day.

"And aren't you the pretty one," he said moving closer and looking her up and down. "Turn around, girl, let's have a good look at you."

Thinking this some standard requirement she hadn't been apprised of, Lilly complied, turning slowly while looking down at the floor.

"Now take that cap off and let's have a look at that pretty hair of yours."

"I don't think I should, sir." She glanced toward the door with a worried look.

"Nonsense! There's no harm in that."

He playfully reached forward, grabbed the duster and tossed it to the other side of the room. He stood in silent admiration as her beautiful blond hair

The Secret of the Spring

broke free, catching the lamplight as she spun away from him.

She darted toward the open the door and was about to flee when she remembered what she had been taught earlier that day. Turning quickly, she said, "Will that be all, sir?"

He smiled and said, "Not by a long shot, my dear – not by a long shot."

But by then she was already closing the door.

He didn't sleep well that night—he couldn't get the girl out of his mind. He dreamt that she had come to him in the middle of the night, then awoke disappointed and frustrated that she wasn't really there.

He realized that he had become obsessed with her and that posed a problem. He was due to leave the hotel in two days' time. If he was going to make his dream a reality there would be no time for the niceties. An immediate, direct, frontal attack with all guns blazing was his only option.

He was still dreaming about her when she materialized in front of him with his breakfast tray in the morning. Setting it down on the night table she moved to pull open the curtains.

As the sunlight hit him, he silently bolstered himself against the pillows and watched as she struggled with the curtain sashes. She glanced toward him and caught his unmoving eyes. His silent stare was unreadable.

Returning to his bedside with her arms outstretched to their full extent, she warily placed the legs of the tray over his lap then quickly stepped back out of his reach. She busied herself tidying the room while he drank his tea and ate his toast.

After he'd finished, still in silence, she cautiously retrieved the tray and headed for the door. She had the tray balanced on one hand and was about to turn the doorknob when he finally spoke.

"Aren't you forgetting something, my dear?" he said, pointing to the white porcelain chamber pot resting under the washstand.

"Oh," she said, "I'm sorry sir, I—, I'm not sure that's part of my duties, but..." She stared at the heavy silver tray and its contents filling her arms. "I'll send someone right up."

She couldn't find Mrs. Stronach so she asked the old chambermaid who also had returned to the kitchen whether it was part of her duties to deal with chamber pots.

"Of course it is, girl," she said, suppressing a smile and giving a conspiratorial wink to the other maids looking up from their work.

When she returned to the room, she found the man standing by the window. His dressing gown was open and hanging loosely over his nightshirt.

"Ah there you are. I thought you were never coming."

He slipped between her and the door, carefully closing it. She went directly to the washstand and picked up the chamber pot with two hands, and turned toward the door.

The Secret of the Spring

"Just a minute, my dear, you're being a bit hasty. Set that pot down for a moment."

She replaced the pot on the bottom shelf of the washstand and stood awkwardly facing it, unsure of what to do next. The young officer moved quickly up behind her, grabbed her by her shoulders, spun her around and kissed her full on the mouth.

She didn't resist, she had been conditioned not to. She simply closed her eyes and drifted off to her special place of safety.

Three hours later Angie found Lilly, dishevelled and glassy-eyed, staggering down the hall with the chamber pot in her hands. Angie took the pot from her, placed it on the floor, wrapped her arms around her and helped her up the stairs to their room.

Lilly couldn't or wouldn't tell what had happened, but she didn't need to—it was plain to see. Angie helped her undress and put on her nightgown, then reached under the bed and pulled out a bottle of the Captain's rum.

"I swiped it from the dining room. I keep it for special occasions, and I think this is one."

She took a long swig herself and then helped Lilly to sit upright and made her sip from the bottle. The girls sat close to each other and shared the liquor until they finished it.

Angie became a little giddy. She started joking and trying to cheer Lilly up, but Lilly had stopped listening or replying. As the rum took its effect, she huddled under the covers and escaped to her special place, unable to speak.

When most of the rum was gone, Angie, assuming that Lilly was asleep, started mumbling with tears in her eyes. "That no good bastard Worthington is sending me home," she moaned, more to herself than to Lilly.

7: A muffled explosive sound

The following day, while Lilly remained in her room, drifting in and out of sleep, the band of sailors gathered on the front stoop, preparing to take their leave. Worthington watched from his office window, frequently looking down at the gold pocket watch he clutched in his hand.

He had been elected to be a one-man mounted escort for the departing party of special guests, but there was something he wanted to be sure of before he had to go to join them. He breathed a sigh of relief and immediately turned to leave after seeing Angie finally emerge, bag in hand, from the lower service door.

By the time he had made his way down to the stable yard where his horse waited, the girl had already disappeared into the woods that surrounded the source of the spring. After he mounted his horse and was securely seated, he dug in his spurs, cantered around to the front of the hotel, caught up to the departing carriage and rode ahead of it.

The Captain, watching the disappearing carriage, sighed with relief. Turning to the next task, he ordered the maids to gather all of the remaining guests together so he could speak to them.

The men and women, summoned from their rooms, the bathhouse, the greens and their games of lawn tennis and croquet, assembled in a curious multitude in front of the hotel. The Captain mounted the steps of the front veranda and began his speech.

"I hope you will forgive me, ladies and gentlemen. It seems that in recent days I have been involved in a plot to deceive you."

His guests looked quizzically at each other and then back to him. "The gentleman whom I allowed you to believe was a simple officer in Her Majesty's Navy was, in fact, the son of that very Queen. For the last few days you have been sharing this hotel with the Prince of Wales!"

The clamour below her window awakened Lilly.

"Angie, is that you?"

"Oh Lil, sorry to wake you—you should try to sleep some more. I was half way up the mountain above the spring when I remembered that I had forgotten these things. Not much, but they're all I have."

"So it wasn't just a bad dream, Angie. You are going! I don't know what I'll do without you. I wish I could come with you."

"I wish you could, too, but we both know that's not possible. So dry those tears, and if there's anything you want to talk about before I go, you better have at it....Lilly, Lilly, are you listening?" *I guess not.* "Well," she whispered, "sleep well, my dearest friend."

Angie bent down, kissed Lilly's forehead, pulled the quilt up around her neck, then shouldered her sling of clothing, headed out the door and down the back stairs for a second and final time.

~

A short while later the train containing the Prince and his crew pulled away from the platform. Worthington mentally patted himself on the back for a job well done, reached into his breast pocket, and discreetly took out his silver flask. Tipping it back, he savoured the few remaining drops, disappointed as usual that the damned thing didn't hold more. *Not to worry*, he thought. There was a whole barrel of smuggled rum waiting for him back in the hotel storeroom.

After a fifteen-minute canter through the increasing darkness, he handed his horse over to the stable man and headed once again to his office. He had just settled down behind his desk when that annoying Mrs. Stronach came knocking at his door with offers of a late supper.

"Thank you so much. The tray looks wonderful. The chef has gone out of his way, and just look at that blueberry pie. But, you know, Mrs. Stronach, I've told you many times that I didn't want you to trouble yourself with attending to these kinds of errands when you have so many eager, youthful legs to do your running for you."

Pox on you, you interfering old bitch, you're always trying to keep me away from those girls.

"Thank you for your concern, Mr. Worthington,

but needs must—we're a little short of maids this evening. As you know, Angeline is no longer with us, Lilly seems to be a little under the weather and the rest of the girls are all busy as bees elsewhere."

"That being the case, Mrs. Stronach, I am even more grateful for this special attention."

I know what you're up to, you jealous old tart, and if I had the stomach for it, I'd accommodate you just for spite.

"Anyway, thank you again and I'm so sorry to hear that Angeline has left us. Oh yes, and give Lilly my best."

Don't bother, you old trollop. If everything works out, she'll be getting my best directly.

"I'd better not take up more of your time, Matron, so off you go."

"Bon appetit, Mr. Worthington."

"Yes, yes, matron. I certainly plan to enjoy everything."

If you only knew, you old bag. Lilly, Lilly, my sweet little Lilly.

Over the next two hours he drank steadily while turning over in his mind the events of the last several days. All in all it had been quite an adventure. Not even the hotels he had served in England had ever played host to royalty. But he, thanks to his efforts, and no thanks to that blustering old Captain Hall, had made it happen. But then that damned interfering Angeline had gone to the Captain with her story about the Prince's dalliance with Lilly and put a cloud on an otherwise capital affair.

The Secret of the Spring

After the Captain had stopped shouting at him, Worthington had agreed to send Angeline packing back to Bear River, where nobody would believe her tale of woe, and the Captain seemed mollified. He didn't realize that Worthington would be killing two birds with one stone, removing the busybody and putting paid to a personal matter of some concern.

Worthington addressed his glass of rum, his long time *confidant*. "Ah, but there remains the matter of our traumatized little Lilly languishing in her room. One more for the road, then I, as her employer, think it behooves me to comfort her. One can do much worse than partake of royal leavings."

Worthington rose unsteadily to his feet, retrieved a lamp from its bracket and staggered out the office door. He made his way down the hall until he reached the entrance to the storeroom, where he fumbled one-handed with the latch for several moments until the door flung inward to reveal the gloomy interior.

He moved to the stairs, then stopped short to test the height of the first step with his foot. Now on familiar territory, he started a slow, drunken ascent.

He had just about reached the top when his foot struck something that startled him. As the cat screeched, he lost his footing and fell backwards.

His flying lamp preceded him the twenty feet to the floor and crashed into shards in a burning pool of oil.

Worthington, back broken and unable to move

other than to crane his neck slightly, watched as fingers of flame flowed toward the stored oil barrels.

At the same time, Angie was down at the spring, remembering the night a year earlier when she had crept over to it to get water for her ailing mother, just as she was doing now. Worthington had discovered her then and, making her feel like a thief, had compelled her to stay and work for him. That was then, but now she knew that he would be more than glad to see the last of her. She would leave willingly, but not without the sacred water she had come for.

As the glass jug burped out its final air and filled, a muffled explosive sound startled Angie. She looked up to see the door that led to the rear storage room of the hotel flung open and the interior ablaze.

Putting down her jug, she ran to the hotel, mounted the steps to the veranda, made her way to the Captain's bell and started frantically ringing it.

When people began to appear and someone relieved her at the bell, she ran through the lobby. She saw the Captain, clutching some papers and a large book, heading for safety. She ran up the stairs, along the hall to the forbidden door to her former room.

Pushing with all her might, she forced the door open and found Lilly standing in her nightgown, barefoot, terrified and confused, holding a lightly singed Yves.

"Angie, Angie, what's happening? What's happening? I didn't know what to do. Look at poor Yves. We've got to help him."

The Secret of the Spring

"Stop crying and worrying about that damned cat, Lilly! Just grab my hand."

Angie dragged Lilly, dressed as she was and cradling the smouldering cat, down through the lobby and out the front door to safety.

A kindly woman on the front lawn produced a blanket and wrapped it around Lilly. Angie took advantage of the growing confusion to slip away to the spring and her jug of precious water.

With her few belongings in one hand and the jug in the other, Angeline turned and began her long walk toward Bear River and home.

Smoke was already hanging like low-slung clouds in the hallways as the staff rousted hotel guests from their beds by furious banging and shouts of "Fire, fire!"

Guests stumbled out of the building, coughing and choking, clad only in their bed clothes. Terrified men and women, many of them barefoot, rushed frantically around the hotel grounds and finally congregated in the pine grove across the road. Someone suggested a bucket brigade, but there were no buckets to be had.

After a time, they heard the sound of galloping hooves as the Middleton Fire Brigade approached. Three spirited grey horses pulled a heavy pumper wagon. The volunteer firemen unhitched the horses and went to work with the pumps and hoses.

But they were too late. The wooden building was already a raging inferno and no amount of water would have had any effect on it. One of the firemen, who had stopped to relieve himself in the direction of the fire, quipped to the man with the hose, "I think I'm doing as much good as you fellas are!"

Guests and members of the staff looked on in horror as the fire lit up the sky and the Spa Springs Hotel burned to the ground.

With one exception, all the guests and staff had made it out of the building before it was consumed. Mr. Worthington, who must have been making sure everyone was safe, had heroically perished.

8: Still on the hook

In the days that followed, departing guests crammed the trains that serviced the Valley. Captain Hall, realizing that he had lost everything, made the quick decision to return to the sea, leaving his staff to fend for themselves.

As the news spread, farm wagons from the families of the jobless hotel servants began arriving at the nearby houses where they had been given temporary shelter. Those who could, returned to their homes on farms up and down the Valley, and others made their way to jobs on the shore, in the woods, or in the mines at Nictaux on the South Mountain.

After Lilly had been with a family for two days and all her fellow workers had been picked up, she realized that her father, who could have seen the distant blaze from his mountain farm and by now must surely heard about it, was not coming for her. Not wishing to impose further, she set off on foot up the mountain in some donated clothes and an old pair of boots. They were no better than the ones she had worn when she had arrived at the hotel.

It took over an hour of walking before she turned into her familiar drive. Her brother Darrel jumped off the front porch and took a few steps in her direction, then quickly turned tail and, arms waving, ran shouting back toward the house.

"Hey Pa! Hey Pa, Lilly's come home!"

Her father was sitting in his familiar place at the table when she entered the kitchen. He looked up at her with blank eyes but said nothing – he'd been drinking again.

She looked at the dirty dishes and the accumulation of clutter and grime that the kitchen had acquired in her absence and, without a word, reached for her old apron, still on the hook, and went to the wood box for kindling for the stove.

9: The smithy's horse

Two months of hard work on Lilly's part had returned the house to a semblance of order. Edgar Leonard's meals had become tolerable again and he was starting to get comfortable with the fact that Lilly was back home.

Sitting in his usual chair at the kitchen table and feeling no pain, he pondered the situation. *Maybe if I keep a watchful eye on those damned boys and have enough rum to calm my nerves, things will work out.*

Taking another swig from the ever present jug, he said aloud to no one in particular, "Yes, by God, I think they will!"

And things did until several days later. He was up early one day, having his usual morning leak out his second story bedroom window, when he noticed Lilly in the distance. She was down on her knees beside the outhouse, throwing up.

He immediately became suspicious and, later, as he had a close look at her hustling around the kitchen getting his breakfast, his fears were confirmed. In spite of all the work she had been doing recently she had put on weight and her apron wasn't totally concealing everything that was happening beneath it.

He wanted to get his whip and beat those bastard boys to death, but first he had some thinking to do, so he yelled at Lilly instead, "Bring me that jug, girl!"

He knew the answer was obvious and no amount of rum was going to change his dilemma, although he gave it a good try. He would have to do what every father in this situation did: find her a husband. *But who the hell can I get to marry a girl, pretty or not, who's going to have a brat fathered by one of her own brothers?*

"Why, God? Why me?" he cried out loud before passing out face down on the table.

Her father hadn't spoken the words, but Lilly could tell from the way he looked at her that he knew. She had known she was pregnant for some time and, after many sleepless nights of anguish, she had decided what she was going to do. She just hadn't decided when.

Now her father had made that decision for her. She must leave before the boys awoke and he had sobered up.

Grabbing her cap from the hook, she opened the door and made her way over the creaky porch boards, leaving her ramshackle home without looking back. She set off down the mountain to find a peaceful spot to end her life. The closest water of any depth was the Annapolis River in the Valley.

The sun rose higher in the sky as she made her way along the gravel road that wound down the slope of the North Mountain. It was becoming oppressively hot.

The Secret of the Spring

She was unusually tired. She had worked hard all her life but she had never felt the kind of fatigue that now seemed to be slowing her steps. *Walking down hill is harder on a person than walking up*, she thought.

She had almost reached the corner where the blacksmith shop stood when she suddenly became very dizzy. She staggered to the side of the road into the shade of some tall pines, intending to rest for a moment. Then everything around her began to spin and she lost consciousness. She fell onto the mossy carpet at base of the trees.

When Lilly came to, she was lying on a daybed behind a wood cookstove in an unfamiliar kitchen. It was about the same size and design as her kitchen on the mountain but it had a neatness and order that, try as she might, she had never been able to maintain at her own home—not with her oafish brothers and father plodding around, never lifting a finger to help her. There were no frills in this place, no lace or fancy work, but everything was clean and fresh smelling.

She could hear two voices: a man's and a woman's and the sound of somebody using the cistern pump. Shortly the woman she only knew vaguely as Mrs. Neilly appeared with a basin of cold water. The plump, grey haired woman knelt at her side and began bathing her forehead. It felt good.

"She's with us again, Ben," she heard the woman say.

After a time the face of the towering blacksmith

appeared over the woman's shoulder. "You fainted, Lilly," he said with concern in his voice. "Were you hurt? Is there anything we can get you?"

"I'm all right, Mr. Johnson, thank you." Trying to sit up, she said, "I'd best be on my way."

"You'll do no such thing," Mrs. Neilly said, pushing her gently down again. "You just lie here and rest a bit while Ben and I decide what's to be done."

Mrs. Neilly took Ben by the arm and directed him out the back door and on to the veranda. She wiped her hands on her apron and looked up the road toward her own house. There was smoke coming from her chimney so, feeling confident that one of her girls was starting supper, she began what she knew would be a lengthy and difficult conversation.

But before she began to speak Ben forestalled her, "Do you think I should go to town and get the doctor?"

She put up her hand to hush him. "You don't need a doctor. I've delivered enough babies to know a pregnant girl when I see one."

Ben wasn't really surprised at what she told him; he had suspected as much. "But she's so young."

"Young or not, it is what it is and there's nothing we can do about it." she replied. "Listen, Ben, there's more to it than that. I was talking to Mrs. Spencer in town the other day. They've been looking after the girl's brother since he lost his eye, and from what the lad said there's been things going on up at that farm. I don't know a nice way of putting this so I'll just come out and say it. The father of this child's baby is

The Secret of the Spring

probably one of her brothers. God knows what's to become of her."

It took Ben a while to digest what he had just heard. Mrs. Neilly watched him as he turned and gripped the veranda railing with his big hands.

As he stared into the distance for what seemed a very long time, his shock turned to anger. "Mrs. Neilly, I think I better go up and talk to her father. Do you suppose you could sit with her while I'm away?"

"Of course. But don't you go doing anything foolish whilst you're up there," she said with a worried look.

"I'll be back as soon as I can."

Ben went to the gate of the little pasture and whistled up his old bay gelding. He bridled him, threw on his old cavalry saddle, mounted and set off up the mountain.

He had only gone a short distance when he detected a ringing sound. *Damn it—a loose shoe*, he thought. *Isn't it always the way—the smithy's horse is the last to get shod*.

Aloud he said, "Sorry, old fellow, I'll look after you as soon as we get back."

He pushed the old horse hard on the way up to the top of mountain, then regretted it when he felt the gelding's flanks heaving and smelt the sweat wafting up from under the saddle. He reined the horse in, rested a while, and then rode the rest of the way to the old Leonard homestead at a slow walk. It gave him time to think and to cool down himself.

The lane to the farm was a tunnel through second

growth cat-spruce and alder bushes. The stone walls on either side of it suggested that the road had once separated two good-sized cleared fields, but after years of neglect the forest was gradually reclaiming them.

Before long the narrow path opened into a clearing where a sway-backed barn and a dilapidated house stood covered in vines. The house must have once been quite grand, but now the fretwork in the eaves was rotting away and the shingles were weathered and curled and large patches of them were missing, exposing areas of bare boards.

As Ben drew closer, two boys leapt up from where they had been lying around in the shade of a big maple by the barn and scurried over to the house.

There was an old seed drill with one broken wheel resting at an odd angle in the dooryard. It looked to be the most substantial object available, so Ben dismounted, looped the horse's reins over the remaining large wooden wheel and headed toward the house.

He was at the top of the porch steps when the battered screen door flew open, sending a half dozen hens squawking and flying in his direction. A glassy-eyed Edgar Leonard stumbled into view, supported on either side by his boys.

"You're a long way from home, Ben," he slurred. "What brings you up on the mountain?"

"Lilly is down at my place and she isn't well. You'd better bring your wagon and get her. She's had enough walking for one day."

"Now what the hell has got into that girl wandering off like that?" Edgar said, turning red in the face. "When I get her home, I'll give her a hiding she won't forget. She won't go bothering folks and embarrassing her family anymore."

He railed on for a while and Ben pretended to listen, but when Edgar said that he wasn't feeling good and that the boys had better take the team and pick up Lilly, Ben raised his hand and called his ranting to a halt.

"I guess maybe you better forget about coming and getting her," he said. "She's better off where she is."

"Just what are you trying to say, Ben Johnson?" Edgar said, tightening his fist and taking a step forward.

"I'll be plain, Edgar. You and your sons are drunken fools and nobody in their right mind would turn that girl over to you."

Edgar lurched forward, aiming a punch in Ben's direction, but the smithy easily deflected the blow and Edgar fell face forward down the porch steps.

As the two brothers rushed at him, all arms and no brains, Ben reached out with his long arms and grabbed them by their hair. He banged their heads together several times before tossing them off the porch on top of their father.

Ben stepped off the porch and stood over the three men, fists clenched, silently daring them to get to their feet, but they had enough sense to remain where they were.

Suppressing the urge to give them a farewell encounter with his boots, Ben went to his horse, mounted and headed slowly back down the mountain.

10: What would people say?

Ben didn't know what he was going to do with the girl, but he did know that, in all good conscience, he couldn't let her go back to that farm.

Maybe Mrs. Neilly would take her in, at least until the child is born, he thought as he rode down into the darkening valley. He hurried the old horse along despite the loose shoe, hoping to reach the forge before night set in.

When his house came into view there was already a lamp burning in the window and smoke coming from the chimney. Mrs. Neilly, who had heard him coming, waited for him on the porch while he unsaddled and turned his horse out into the pasture. Resetting the old horse's shoes would be first on his list of jobs at the forge come morning.

He climbed the steps and looked past his neighbour through the open door to where he could see Lilly still lying on the daybed behind the stove.

Mrs. Neilly bided her time. She ushered him inside, saying, "I've got the coffee on and I found some fixings to make a stew. It should be about ready to eat. Why don't you sit down and I'll fetch you a plate?"

"Thanks, but I'm not really hungry. Maybe the girl—?"

"Best let her be for a while, Ben. I'll get us some coffee and we can talk on the porch."

Cups in hand, they took chairs on the porch, but neither one could sit easy. Mrs. Neilly made a production of blowing the steam away from her cup. Then she said, without looking at Ben, "I take it her father isn't coming for her."

"No, he isn't!"

"So what's to be done with her?"

"Well, I was hoping you could take her in for a spell. I would pay for her keep, and maybe after the child is born—"

"Now you hold on right there, Ben Johnson. I don't want to sound mean but there is no way I can have that girl in my house in her condition, and knowing what I know about her situation. I've got three girls of my own to think about, and my old man wouldn't stand for it, either. There are places for girls like her. She could go up to the Poor Farm near Aylesford."

"The Poor Farm," Ben said slowly.

"They'll look after her there. I'll send one of my girls over to sit with her tonight. I can't let her stay alone with you—what would people say? You can ride to town in the morning and get Reverend McKay to come and get her. He usually deals with these things."

Ben didn't argue with her; there didn't seem any point to it.

When Mrs. Neilly's daughter arrived later on, he

The Secret of the Spring

grabbed a blanket, went out to the barn and made a bed for himself in the hay up in the loft. It would just have to do for now.

Ben didn't sleep well that night. He had a recurring nightmare that had haunted him ever since childhood. He woke in a cold sweat and it was moments before he realized that he wasn't still a child back in that terrible London workhouse.

He lay awake for the remainder of the night, and by the time the sun started streaming through the loft door he had made up his mind. The girl wouldn't be going anywhere.

He lingered in the barn, watching the yard so he could speak to Mrs. Neilly before she went into the house to relieve her daughter.

When he told her that he planned to let the girl stay with him until he could find a suitable family to take her in, she couldn't believe her ears. "What are you thinking? You can't do that."

"Don't waste a lecture on me. My mind is determined."

Eventually, she went to the house and got her daughter. The two of them marched away, washing their hands of the matter.

When Ben entered the kitchen, Lilly was sitting up on the cot, sipping a cup of coffee. She looked up at him timidly as he pulled one of the kitchen chairs over close to her and sat down.

"I was up to see your father yesterday and I didn't like what I saw up there. You can't go back. Mrs. Neilly can't take you in, neither. She thinks you should go to the county home. I know what those places are like and I don't want you to go there. I don't know how to arrange it properly but I think you should stay here."

Since Lilly only intended to stay until she could manage to slip away and continue her trip to the river, she simply nodded a silent yes into her cup.

Ben told her where things were in the kitchen so that the girl could feed herself and, cup in hand, he headed off to the forge.

News travelled fast in the Valley but, although many of the men who brought their horses to be shod that day were aware of the girl's presence in the house, none of them felt comfortable addressing the subject with Ben. When he went back to the house around noon, he found Lilly washing the dishes that had accumulated since Mrs. Neilly's departure.

"You shouldn't be up doing that," he said. Taking her gently by the arm, he steered her back to her cot.

When his day was finished, Ben returned to the house to find the dishes done, the table set and his supper in the warming oven. The girl was nowhere to be seen, and when he called her name there was no answer.

He was about to run out to the yard to look for her when the door to the woodshed and the outhouse opened slowly and the girl appeared. He watched her cross the bare yard to the house with her head down and her arms folded.

Without saying anything Lilly went to the stove,

The Secret of the Spring

got his plate and placed it on the table. Ben brought his chair up to the table, got another from beside the wall and placed it on the opposite side of the table.

"Sit down, girl. Where's your plate?"

"I'm not hungry, thanks, sir. I ate some earlier."

"Well, sit down anyway, Lilly, it's been a long time since I had anyone joining me at this table."

Ben carried on a one way conversation with the girl, only getting an occasional 'yes' or 'no' out of her as he spoke of his day and plied her with carefully-worded questions.

When he finished his meal, he looked for a moment at the uncomfortable cot behind the stove. "Lilly, take those blankets off the cot and run them up to the empty room at the top of the stairs. You'll be more comfortable up there."

For a moment Lilly felt her mind slipping away to her special place, but when he spoke again the thought faded.

"I'll be heading out to the barn now and I'll see you in the morning."

Ben had seen the distressed look on the girl's face and he knew what she must have been thinking. He paused at the door. "I see a dirty dish distresses you, so I won't say you should not wash up. You should do what gives you ease."

In the barn, Ben spread out his blankets and settled down on the hay by the open loft door, where he could see the house. After a while he watched the small orb of candlelight glide past the kitchen windows, disappear for a moment as the girl made her way up the stairs and reappear in the bedroom window. Lilly's shadow was cast on the opposing bedroom wall, and then the light went out.

In those sparse moments he had found her presence strangely comforting. With the sudden return of darkness however, the seriousness of the situation struck him again. *This arrangement can't go on forever. There must be some kind soul who could take the girl in.*

No suitable person or family immediately sprang to mind and he was still going over possibilities when he drifted off to sleep.

11: What terrible sinners we are

Ben wasn't himself the following day as he went about his work at the forge. He only listened with half an ear to the conversations buzzing around him. He had performed the familiar tasks so often that he could have accomplished them in his sleep and that was just as well because his mind constantly drifted back to the girl in his kitchen.

Mrs. Neilly had changed her mind and agreed to sit with Lilly while he was at work in the forge, and he was grateful. If only she would stop harping at him, trying to talk him into sending her to the Poor Farm.

He was going over and over all the families he knew, trying to come up with a suitable couple that might be able to take her in when he heard a snatch of conversation that caught his attention.

Spurgeon Adams was making his annual appeal for help with the apple harvest at Hillfoot Farm. "I tell you, boys, you'll never find a better place to work. Miss Stirling pays the best wages in the Valley and the company ain't too bad there, either. She's got all them boys and girls that she brought from Scotland and others from around here helping in the orchard, and there're quite a few older fillies there that ain't all that hard on the eyes."

Ben wondered why he hadn't thought of it before. He had even been to the place a couple of times in the past, delivering parts he'd repaired for the steam engine that powered their sawmill.

As soon as he finished for the day he went to the house and took Mrs. Neilly aside. "I know it's a big favour to ask, but could you stay with Lilly again tomorrow? I want to go and see Miss Stirling at her place near Aylesford. I'm thinking that her home at Hillfoot Farm might be a good safe place for the girl to stay for a while. It's a long way up to Welton Corner and it will take most of the day."

"I don't know much about that place, Ben, other than that the woman who runs it is not a Baptist—she's one of them Presbyterians."

"Yes, I'll grant you that, but in spite of that she might still be a good woman—so what do you say?"

"It is indeed a lot to ask. I have an awful pile of work waiting for me at home."

He didn't say more; just looked steadily at her until she looked away.

"Oh, well, your intentions are the best for that girl....I guess I can give you one more day. Here's hoping it won't be a waste, on both our parts. Oh, that poor child!"

The next morning Ben set out early. The trip along the Valley floor wouldn't take too long, as his destination was just ten miles away. With any luck he could meet with Miss Stirling and easily be home in time

The Secret of the Spring

for the supper he was sure Mrs. Neilly would have waiting for him.

As he trotted along he passed lumbering teams of oxen hauling long wagons laden with heavy barrels and puncheons. The apple harvest was in full swing and the orchards along the way were teeming with activity: men, women and children hanging off flimsy ladders filled their baskets with the red and golden fruit.

He recognized and acknowledged several people he knew, the opportunities and requirements to return waves and nods diminishing the further he got from home. Ten miles could be two, three or even four communities along and not many people ventured out of their local neighbourhood unless for some extreme event.

After nearly two hours of steady travel he passed the road that led up and over the mountain to the seaside village of Morden, and shortly thereafter Hillfoot Farm came into view. The place had grown since he last saw it. The old farmhouse had expanded tenfold and there were new barns and outbuildings nicely situated around the property. The sawmill he had worked on had been put to good use, milling out the logs that had come from the forest up on the North Mountain.

He turned his horse into the dooryard of the main house, climbed down from the buggy and tied his horse to the nearby hitching pole.

"Ah, Mr. Johnson," Miss Stirling declared as one of her charges ushered him into her private sitting room. "And what is it that brings you so far from home today? It can't be for more repairs on the mill. Mr. Keddy tells me the parts you fixed have been performing admirably."

Ben, cap in hand, glanced over his shoulder—the girl who'd escorted him in was still standing in the doorway. Sensing his discomfort, Miss Stirling dismissed her with a wave of her hand.

"Thank you," Ben said, shifting from foot to foot and twisting his cap.

After giving the state of his clothes and shoes a quick appraisal, Miss Stirling nodded toward a velvet-upholstered chair and invited him to sit. "Now tell me, what's on your mind, Mr. Johnson. I assume it's a matter of some delicacy." With a forced smile on her face, she added, "Let me assure you that over the years of running this establishment I have seen and heard it all, and very little shocks me."

"That's just as well," Ben said and proceeded to tell her how he had come to have a pregnant fifteen-year-old girl lodging with him. He thought it might injure her chances of being accepted if he mentioned her involvement with her brothers, so he left out that portion of the sordid tale.

The old spinster, whose smile was gradually dissolving into a frown, listened attentively until he finished. They sat staring at each other for a full minute before she spoke.

"I told you that I had heard it all, Mr. Johnson, and I have, and I must tell you that your story is a familiar one. I have heard it countless times before, both

The Secret of the Spring

here and in Scotland. Always the same: a man with a cock-and-bull story about how some girl has become mysteriously pregnant and although he bears absolutely no responsibility, would like to see her properly looked after. I thought better of you, Ben Johnson, I must say, but I'll tell you what I have told hundreds before you: I will not turn the girl away—I never have and I never will. But, you, my man, are not getting off Scot-free. You will be required to pay for her keep as long as she is with me and to continue to do so until I'm able to find a suitable situation for her."

Ben stood up. "You don't understand, Miss Stirling, I really—"

"Not another word!" she said. With an angry gesture, she picked up a small bell from the end table and rang it loudly. "Esther will show you around the home, and if you are amenable to the conditions I have proposed, you may bring the girl to us. Oh and yes, please send your payments by mail as I have no wish to ever see you again."

Ben made several attempts to explain himself, but each time Miss Stirling put up her hand and shushed him as if he were a grammar school boy. He felt like choking the arrogant bitch, but instead simply followed Esther when she reappeared, leaving matters as they stood.

He had no intention of taking the tour. When he and the girl reached the hall, he plopped his cap on and made to leave.

But she leaned into him and whispered, "Please walk with me a bit or I'll get into trouble."

She took him into the dining hall, and after looking around to be sure no one was near, began in a hushed voice, "I know you, Ben—sometimes I went to your shop with my father. I heard what you said to Miss Stirling. Please don't send that girl here unless you really have to. It may look nice, but it's not all it's cracked up to be. I wish I could get away. It's clean and there's plenty of food but we're all puppets and that old bag pulls the strings. If she hasn't got us looking after the little ones, doing the laundry, working in the kitchen or slaving away in the fields and orchards, we're sitting in that damned chapel listening to what terrible sinners we are."

Tears were flowing down her cheeks now. "And she takes our babies away and gives them to whoever she chooses."

With that, the girl darted away and Ben was left to find his own way out.

Before he had travelled a mile toward home he had made up his mind. It wasn't just what the young girl had said. He could have lived with the disgrace of being thought a lecher and wouldn't have minded paying for Lilly's keep—he had little else to spend his money on. It was something else, something that had haunted him for years, a dark memory of the place he had been confined in as a five-year-old child.

He clucked the horse on and then changed his mind and slowed him to a walk again. Supper would be waiting, but he wasn't in a hurry to confront Mrs. Neilly with his decision. She would not be pleased.

And for sure, she didn't disappoint him. As soon as she heard his plans, she let loose with a thorough tongue lashing and then, resisting the temptation to throw his supper at him, stormed home.

12: Enough is enough

Later that night Ben was startled awake by the sound of someone pounding on the door of his house across the yard. He swung the loft door open and saw Mrs. Neilly standing on his porch, a lantern in one hand and a struggling Lilly by her wrist in the other.

Ben hailed her from the loft and once she spied him, she turned and shouted, "Ben Johnson, you get down here this minute!"

Ben pulled on his boots, straightened his shirt and headed for the house.

"Get in that kitchen and stay there!" he heard her shout at the girl as he approached. Then she turned on him.

"Enough is enough, Ben. My man found this girl walking the roads tonight and dragged her home to me."

"I'm sorry, Mrs.—"

"My husband is not the brightest penny in the pouch, but even he has more sense than you. He says the only answer is to go for Reverend McKay."

Ben held up his hand. "I told you she wasn't going to the Poor Farm." he declared with finality.

"I'm not talking about any old Poor Farm," she in-

The Secret of the Spring

sisted. "I'm talking about getting the preacher out here to get the pair of you hitched."

"Are you crazy? I'm old enough to be her grandfather. Even if I agreed to your hair-brained idea, the girl would never consent."

"She hasn't got much choice. And if you're hellbent on helping her, you don't, either. So be quiet and stay out here while I go talk to her."

Mrs. Neilly spent the better part of an hour talking to Lilly in the kitchen before she returned to Ben, pleased with herself. "Yes, your young bride says, so that's settled."

She didn't realize that it wasn't her power of persuasion that got the girl to agree. Lilly still planned to escape and make her way to the river. Whatever happened to her over the next few days would only temporarily delay the inevitable.

The following evening Mr. and Mrs. Neilly arrived in Ben's dooryard in a democrat buggy, with a stern and unhappy-looking Reverend McKay in the back seat.

Ben and Lilly were waiting in the parlour for them. Lilly was wearing a flowered frock that one of the Neilly girls had loaned her and Ben was dressed in a suit that had seen better times. The Neillys would serve as witnesses and, as the preacher put it, the bride's parental approval will be taken as a given.

Reverend McKay knew that the parties involved didn't want a fuss, so he didn't create one. The ceremony was his short version, just enough words to make it legal. However he couldn't resist the opportunity to show his contempt for the situation. After declaring them man and wife, he said in a forbidding tone, "You may kiss the bride."

Ben wanted to hit the man but instead he leaned over and gave Lilly a tight-lipped peck on the top of her head.

The wedding party was not in the mood for celebration, so Ben simply paid the Reverend's inflated fee and escorted him out to the Neillys' buggy. While Mr. Neilly made the return trip to town, Mrs. Neilly laid out a special wedding supper that she and her girls had prepared. They would not be sharing it with the newlyweds. They felt Ben and Lilly should be left alone, so with minimal ceremony, they all said their goodbyes and walked home.

The food provided was excellent but it was probably the most uncomfortable meal that either Ben or Lilly had ever eaten. They both picked at their food and Ben made a few attempts at conversation but Lilly was unresponsive. He knew she was worrying about what might happen to her now that they were married.

Ben didn't want to prolong her anxiety. "Now then," he said. "I think we understand that things should continue as they have begun. So I'm off to the barn for the night." He stood up from the table and pushed his chair back.

Almost as a second thought, he reached in his pocket and pulled out a small package. "I guess you better wear this." Then he headed out the door.

The Secret of the Spring

Lilly opened the package to reveal the most beautiful thing she had ever seen: a solid gold ring, gleaming in the lamplight, wider and heavier than a normal wedding band and etched with the images of tiny deer-like creatures loping around its perimeter. It wasn't really a wedding ring, not anything like the slim plain bands that Lilly had seen on other women.

In the barn, Ben made his bed ready and stretched out on it, remembering the events that had led up to his acquiring the ring in Africa. Soldier's plunder. He thought of his regiment, and of things that they had done that nobody who had not been there would believe or want to hear.

In the house, Lilly was forcing herself to wake from an unintended nap. She was planning to slip away again, but feeling the weight of the wonderful ring on her finger, she considered the kindness of the man who had given it to her. She turned the ring slowly, looking at the prancing creatures, and at some point she changed her mind.

It wasn't because she was happy in the big man's company. She couldn't remember being truly happy anywhere, certainly not at her home. There were those few moments at the hotel in Angeline's company but that was almost over before it began.

She didn't understand Ben and didn't know what to expect from him or what he expected from her, but something truly unexpected was happening, something she had never experienced before. She was beginning to feel safe.

It was probably just an illusion and would disappear or be spoiled or taken away—she was tired, too tired, to think about it anymore. For now, she was content to stay put.

Another day or two here won't make much difference, she thought.

13: The unlikely couple

A couple of days turned into weeks, and weeks into months. The unlikely couple became real friends. Ben made no demands on Lilly and she in turn did everything she could to please him: cooking, cleaning, darning, mending and any other household chore that presented itself.

During the first few weeks she went about her chores silently, only answering him when he spoke to her, never initiating any conversation. That changed one evening when Ben decided to re-read one of the books he kept on a shelf in the kitchen. As he opened it he felt the girl move in close behind him, sharing the light of his lamp.

"What's it about?" Lilly asked, with real interest in her voice.

Turning his head so he could see her face, he said, "It's about an orphan boy named Pip. The book's called *Great Expectations*. You can read it if you like."

He closed the book and held it out toward her, but she had stepped back out of the circle of lamplight. "I can't read," he heard her say from the darkness.

Ben was shocked and speechless. *What a fool I am*, he thought. *I should have known.*

As he heard the girl moving away from him, he said, "Would you like me to read some of it to you?"

There was a short pause, and then, together with the sound of another chair being pulled up to the table, he heard, "I'd like that very much, Ben."

It's Ben now! he thought as he opened the book and began with the first words, "'My father's name being Pirrup and my Christian name Philip, my infant tongue could make of both names nothing longer or more explicit than Pip.'"

He read on into the night. Two hours later, when he started to get drowsy, Lilly and Ben left Pip wondering if the sergeant was going to arrest him. Ben headed to the barn, promising to continue the story the following evening.

The next morning while she served him breakfast, Lilly was full of questions about the book. She spoke of the characters as if they were real people and plied him with questions about what was going to happen next.

He put her off, saying, "You'll just have to wait and see."

And so a nightly ritual began, with Ben reading and Lilly sitting at his side. Partway through the evening on the second night, they came to pages with etched illustrations. Lilly moved in closer to see them. From then on, whenever he read, they shared the small flickering sphere of lamplight.

A few days after Ben began his nightly readings, he came into the kitchen to find Lilly still working at the table making pie crusts. As he watched her tiny fingers clutching the rolling pin he noticed that she wasn't wearing the ring he had given her. Feeling

The Secret of the Spring

slightly offended by its absence, he tried to sound casual when he inquired, "What have you done with that old ring of yours, Lil?"

"It's in a safe place upstairs, Ben. It's so beautiful and I'm always afraid I'm going to lose it when I'm working around the house or digging in the garden. I feel like it still belongs to you and you've been so good to me—I wouldn't want anything to happen to it."

"Now you listen to me, girl. I gave you that ring and I mean for you to keep it. But it does show good sense that you don't want to wear out working around the place, so, if you like, next time I'm in town I'll get a good sturdy necklace for you to hang it on. I wouldn't want you to lose it, either. I've carried that ring around with me for a long time."

Knowing full well that he had never done it, he said, "Did I ever tell you how I came to have the thing?"

Quickly Lilly wiped the flour from her hands on her apron and settled down in a chair to listen. Then she jumped up again. "No—wait 'til I get it, Ben, and then tell me the story."

She ran upstairs and shortly reappeared with the ring on her finger She showed it to him with a smile, then settled into her chair.

"I don't really know where to start, but I suppose the beginning is as good a place as any," Ben said. "When I was in the 17th Lancers—that's a British cavalry unit—I was what you call a Farrier Sergeant. That's quite a fancy name for a blacksmith, but they have to give that rank to anyone who's handy with shoeing horses if they want to keep him for long. There are those that say the Farrier Sergeant is the most important man in the regiment. I guess it's because if you 'got no shoes, you got no horse.' Horses can't travel far or fast barefoot."

Ben then digressed for a moment and stood up while he quoted an old verse:

> For want of a nail, the shoe was lost.
> For want of a shoe, the horse was lost.
> For want of the horse, the rider was lost.
> For want of a rider, the message was lost.
> For want of the message, the battle was lost.
> For want of a battle, the kingdom was lost.
> And all for the want of a horseshoe nail.

Feeling rather proud of himself, he stood there for a moment hoping for a sign of approval from Lilly. Nothing! So, he sat back down and took up his story again.

"Anyway, in the late fall of 1878 we Lancers shipped out for South Africa. The boys in the Infantry over there were having trouble with a bunch of natives they called Zulus. We left the dock in early December and never touched land again until we landed at the Cape three weeks later. I spent most of my time below decks seeing to the horses. Only about half the poor buggers made it. We fed the rest to the sharks as we moved down the west coast of Africa. After we got to Cape Town we rested up a bit and found some local horses to replace the ones we lost. Then we headed north with a column to a place called Rorke's Drift."

At this point Ben stopped his story and initiated a custom that he and Lilly would continue for the rest of time they spent together.

"Get me that big red leather book over there on the shelf and I'll show you something."

She lugged it to the table and set it down carefully in front of him.

"This is what you call an atlas, Lilly. It's got maps of every place in the world."

He opened the old book and turned to the page that held the map of Africa and pointed out the places he was telling her about. Then he continued his story.

14: Pleading eyes

"The British had had a hell of a scrap with the Africans," Ben began. "This would have been back in 1879. And when they looked like they were about licked, the officer sent us boys in the 17th charging into them to chase them back to their compound. I think they called it a kraal. I don't like remembering what we did with our lances and sabres that day— it was a bloody mess.

"I made it all the way to the centre of the village inside the enclosure and right up to the main hut that their king used. I got off my horse, drew my sabre and headed careful-like inside. The place looked to be deserted. The king, a fella called Cetshwayo, was already gone.

"It was the strangest place I ever saw—just a grass hut, really, but in the middle of all sorts of things in there was a brand new American-made cookstove and a full length mirror on a mahogany stand!

"I was just about finished snooping around and was heading out to see how the rest of the fellas were doing when I saw movement in a pile of hides against one wall. I stepped over to it and used the tip of my sword to lift the top skin. I guess I thought I was going to find the king inside but what I found was a beautiful young black girl crouched into a ball, looking totally terrified. Judging from what was happening to the women in the compound just outside, her fear was justified.

"We stared at each other for a while and then I lowered my sword. She must have been one of the king's wives and had been too slow in escaping. As she looked up at me with pleading eyes I gestured for her to stay put.

"When I went to throw the hide over her again and she realized that I wasn't going to hurt her, she raised her hand and stopped me. She took that very ring off her finger and handed it to me.

"Maybe I shouldn't have accepted it, but I did. I covered her up again and headed back out of the hut.

"That's when it happened: a stray bullet caught me on the side of my head and I blacked out. I don't know how long I was out, but when I finally woke up and came to my senses, I was on a hospital ship headed home. I found the ring with the rest of my things in my kit bag.

"So there you go, Lilly. Your ring once belonged to a princess. From one princess to another," he said, smiling.

Lilly held up her hand and stared at the treasure on her finger. Then she looked at Ben. "But you were somewhere far away when you got this. How did you end up here?"

"That's a story for another day, girl," he replied.

15: Not my London

"Whew! I'm just about talked out!" Ben declared after reading the first two chapters of 'A Christmas Carol' non-stop.

"Oh please, Ben, we can't leave it there. Just a little bit more?"

Bribed with a fresh cup of tea, Ben agreed to a few more pages. But while she was pouring it, an idea occurred to him and without thinking, he let it tumble out. "Lilly, how would you like to learn to read? I could teach you."

The girl sat silent, as if unsure of what to say. "I don't think I could, Ben. I don't think I'm smart enough. They wouldn't take me at the school. The teacher had my brothers there for a while but just sent them home. She said there was no hope for them. She told my father not to bother sending any more Leonards; it was just a waste of time."

"That's a bunch of nonsense. You're a clever girl and I know I can have you reading and writing in no time at all. We're going to make a start tomorrow."

"Oh, Ben, you'll just get mad at me. I know I'm too dumb. I know I am."

"It's like this, young lady: you will try or I'll stop reading this book and you'll never find out what happens to Mr. Scrooge and Tiny Tim."

Lilly pouted but finally agreed to give it a try.

When he was done at the forge the following day, Ben entered the kitchen armed with an old slate and chalk he'd found in the attic. He plopped them down on the table where Lilly could see them while they ate their supper.

When they had finished their meal Lilly rushed to the bookshelf and retrieved 'A Christmas Carol', pulling out the scrap of poplin she used as a page marker and opening it where they'd left off the night before.

"Not so fast, my dear, first things first," he said, shoving the book aside. He pulled the slate in close to him and said, "Now, you bring your chair in beside me and we'll get started. First I'm going to teach you your letters."

Feigning reluctance, she moved her chair in close to him, sat down and said, "So what's the first one?"

"A," he replied.

"I said 'what's the first letter I got to learn?'" she repeated.

Understanding her confusion and more than a little amused, he repeated what he had said, this time with more emphasis on what had seemed like a question to her. "Aye."

"Are you going deaf? I said, 'what's the first letter I need to learn?'"

Ben burst out laughing and was a full minute before he got control of himself. When he could speak again he patted her hand and said, "No, my dear, the first letter is called an 'A' and it looks like this."

When he released her hand to draw the letter on the slate, she jumped up out of her chair and stepped back away from him. Her blue eyes misted over and she sobbed, "If you're just going to make fun of me, you can keep your slate and your old books. I told you I was stupid and couldn't learn." As her tears began, she turned and ran up the stairs to her room.

Ben sat for a confused moment before he hurried to the foot of the stairs and called up to her, "Lilly, Lilly, I'm sorry. I didn't mean to hurt your feelings. If you come down, I promise I won't tease anymore."

He waited for a minute and when there was no reply he decided to sweeten the pot. "If you come down we can read a chapter before we start again."

He waited and when she still didn't respond, he had an inspiration and went over to the table and retrieved the book. He moved back to the stairwell and in his booming baritone voice, began to read, "'Awaking in the middle of a prodigiously tough snore, and sitting up in bed to get his thoughts together, Scrooge had no occasion to be told that the clock was again upon the stroke of one.'"

He read on at the top of his voice, listening in the silences between the pages for any response. When he thought he detected movement above him he backed a short distance away and lowered his voice a little and continued to read.

He repeated this procedure several times, inching his way back to his chair at the table. By the time he was seated and was reading in his normal speaking

The Secret of the Spring

voice, Lilly had tiptoed first to her doorway, then step by step down the stairs and was now listening just out of sight.

The donkey has followed the carrot, Ben thought with satisfaction but stifled the urge to say it out loud.

For twenty minutes he continued to read page after page, finishing with, "'Scrooge hung his head to hear his own words quoted by the Spirit, and was overcome with penitence and grief.'" Ben slammed the book shut and cast a glance toward the doorway just in time to see one of Lilly's dainty little feet being pulled back out of sight

Getting up with a huge stretch and a yawn, he said, "Well, I'm off to my bed, Lil. We'll try again tomorrow and I promise I'll behave myself. Sleep well, girl." He headed to the barn hoping he had made amends.

The following day all was forgiven and the first lesson went extremely well. Ben was astonished at how quickly the girl absorbed what he was teaching her. Within the week Lilly was proudly printing her name, and whenever Ben ventured into the kitchen during the days that followed, he would find evidence of her dogged perseverance on the old slate and the scraps of birch bark they were using in lieu of precious paper.

Within two months Lilly was writing short sentences and reading snippets of text that a proud Ben provided for her.

One evening Lilly didn't bring the book they had

been reading to the table after supper. Instead she simply settled down in her chair with her hands clasped, staring at Ben.

"What is it, girl — where's our book?" he asked.

"You remember back when you said you'd tell me how you came to be here in the Valley? Well, when you tell me stories about yourself it sounds a lot like the ones in the books. So tell me how it all happened that you ended up so far from your Africa, Ben. The book can wait."

Ben was flattered but not sure how to begin. Since she had become inquisitive he had thought a lot about what he should share with her about his life. At first he thought he would avoid the bad things that had happened to him and give her a sugar-coated version, but then he realized that nothing that had happened to him was likely to shock or trouble a girl who had been through what she had. If he was going to tell it to her, he was going to tell it the way it really was. Strangely this young snip of a girl was the first person in his life he felt safe and comfortable enough with to share his story.

"Well, girl," he said, "if I am going to tell you about where I've been and what I've done so that you'll understand, we're going to need that atlas again."

Lilly went to the shelf and brought the now-familiar book to the table. Ben thumbed through the index and finding the page number, opened the book at a map of the British Isles.

"Come sit beside me, girl, so you can see." He plopped a finger at a spot on a river and then asked her to read the place name. She tried once then hesitated and looked to him for help.

"Just sound it out, Lilly—you can do it."

Slowly she put the letters together until they formed the name, "L-on-don?"

"That's it, Lil, that's the place where I was born—London, England. It is the largest city in all of the British Isles and it's the capital. That's where Buckingham Palace is, where the Queen of England lives. I was born in London and later I went to Africa where that girl princess gave me your ring."

He flipped a page over and revealed an etching of the city of London. It was a glorified rendition viewed from some point that included all the best aspects of the city. Lilly began asking questions about the picture and Ben found himself identifying Westminster Abbey, the Houses of Parliament, St. Paul's Cathedral, the Tower, Buckingham Palace and a host of other places before he finally stopped the girl's questions by slamming the book closed.

Lilly was startled, but Ben began immediately to explain himself. "You see, Lilly, that was London, but not my London."

16: The clang of a hammer

"I never went to any of those wonderful places. I lived with my mother in one room in a shabby hovel by a river called the Thames. No artist would have been interested in sketching where we lived. I never knew who my father was.

"My mother, while she was still alive, got close to some of those places when she walked to a place called Covent Garden. There was a big market there and she helped a woman who sold vegetables at the market, but I never went with her. When I was very young a neighbour woman watched me while my Mum was away. The woman put up with me in exchange for a share of the overripe vegetables my mother would bring home—they were part of her wages.

"I was with the neighbour woman one afternoon when a bobby—a policeman, I mean—appeared at the door with the news that a carthorse had run my mother down in the street and she was dead. I was five years old at the time.

"I stayed with the neighbour woman for a day or two while she arranged for someone to come and take me to a home. The man picking me up asked for any bits of clothing and personal things I might have but the women said I only had what was on my back and that wasn't much. She had children of her own who were my size and I guess she figured I wouldn't need much where I was going. She did show a bit of compassion as I was going out the door because she stopped us and shoved a tiny tintype of my mother into my hand.

"The man dropped me off at an orphanage and it was a horrible, horrible place. After the big oak front door slammed shut behind me, I never saw the light of day for about three months. I think it must have been worse than a prison. It sure seemed like one.

"It felt like there were hundreds of boys of all ages crammed into that place and I was left to fend for myself, just five years old. We ate and spent most of our time in one big long room that looked like it might once have been a stable, and we all slept in another about the same size. There was a row of bunk beds crammed against each wall, with barely enough room to slip between them. The lucky boys, the bigger ones, got the bunks but we smaller fellas had to make do with the spaces on the floor between the beds.

"When you first arrived, they shaved your head to keep the lice away and gave you a blanket. The haircut didn't stop the lice; it just slowed them down a bit. The bigger boys stole the blankets from the little kids so they had two blankets each and us smaller ones were forced to share, sometimes two or three to a blanket.

"Our food was mainly gruel for breakfast and a thin, terrible stew for supper. It was mostly water with a bit of cabbage and turnip thrown in. I can abide cabbage, but every time I taste or even smell a turnip, I remember that terrible place. The only good thing about that awful stuff was that it tasted so bad that nobody wanted to steal it from you.

"We also got a bit of bread now and then around midday. The home had an arrangement with several bakeries to take their stale loaves. If you didn't mind a little blue mould, it was a welcome treat. It was more than nothing, that's for sure.

"The nights were the worst time at the place. During the day there was a woman who we had to call Matron who supervised the place, but at night a man who was moonlighting at a second job took charge. Although he was supposed to be awake and patrolling his whole shift, he hardly ever made it through half the night before kicking a boy out of a lower bunk, taking his place and snoring the rest of the night.

"During the first part of the night, once all the staff had left, the man would receive visitors—older men, well-dressed toffs who preferred the company of little boys to that of women. After settling his visitors in another room he would come into the dormitory and select a boy and lead him out. Sometimes he would return quickly and angrily throw the boy back into the room and choose another one, but most of the time, whatever boy was chosen was gone for a long time and we often heard screams echoing through the halls.

The Secret of the Spring

"Whenever that ogre came into the dormitory, I pulled my blanket over my head and tried to hide.

"It worked for a while, but one night one of the older boys was sent back and told to send someone younger. He yanked my blanket from me and pushed me toward the door.

"Our night supervisor was waiting for me. He grabbed my arm and led me down the hall. We went to a room I had never been in before.

"A grey-haired man was sitting in a wing-backed chair, holding a top hat on his lap. I was made to stand in front of him while the supervisor stripped my clothes off. When I tried to cover myself, the supervisor pulled my hands away. The man just stared at me for a long time, but when he made a move to get up and touch me, the supervisor stopped him. He told him he had only paid to look, not touch. The man reached into his jacket for his wallet, but the supervisor told him there wasn't enough time left that evening. If he returned the following night and brought enough cash with him, something could surely be arranged.

"Before he sent me back to the dormitory, the supervisor found me another blanket—I guess he didn't want to take a chance on his goods being damaged. I checked to see that my mother's picture was still in my shirt pocket before I wrapped myself in the blanket and cried myself to sleep. I still have that old picture of my mother. It's that one over there on the shelf."

Ben was silent for a long time, but Lilly knew he

wasn't done. She sat as still as she could, barely breathing.

After a bit, Ben moved his shoulders a little, took a deep breath, and brought his attention back into the room. "The home was just a temporary stop for boys like me. They were in the business of putting us out, selling us, really, to families and businesses that needed cheap help. I got lucky. I might have ended up working in one of the factories or, because of my size, being apprenticed to a chimney sweep. Early in the morning, as I hung around with the other boys in the dining hall, Matron led a huge man in a slouch cap and grimy clothes over to me. I had noticed him looking over the room when he first arrived. He stood there having a closer look at me for a moment or two and then asked my name. When I told him it was Ben, he seemed surprised and moved—I found out why later on.

"He went away with Matron for a brief period, came back, took my hand and led me away. No one told me who he was or where I was going. I was terrified, remembering what had happened the night before. I felt like running away, but he held onto me with his huge hand and there was no chance.

"We walked through the streets for what seemed like ages until we finally came to a house with a large shed on the side. The door to the shed was open and I could hear the clang of a hammer on an anvil and see a fire glowing deep in its interior. There were horses tethered nearby.

"The big man shouted something into the shed

and then dragged me up the back steps to the house. The door swung open and there was a large, wholesome-looking woman in an apron.

"She stood staring at me for a short time. Then she knelt down, wrapped her arms around me and started crying. I can still hear the man laughing and asking her if she thought I would do.

"The man was called Big Lloyd. I found out later that Lloyd and Meg Dexter had lost their only son a couple of years earlier. He would have been about my age, and had the same name as me. Although Lloyd had plans for me in his smithy, I was also destined to fill a void in their family."

Lilly got to her feet, went over and picked up the picture of Ben's mother. She stared at it for a minute. She had seen it before but had never known who it was.

When she returned to the table, she had tears in her eyes.

"Now, now, Lilly, it wasn't all bad."

Garry Leeson

17: Who could teach me the most

Ben seemed to be moving into a less-painful part of his story. "Lloyd Dexter ran one of the largest smithies in London. He and his assistants turned out ironwork and shod hundreds of horses in the course of a week. His shop held the London record, shoeing eighty-three horses in one ten-hour workday.

"After a couple of days of coddling from Meg, I made my way out to the shop and started hanging around and watching. Lloyd found odd jobs to keep me out of mischief. He put me in charge of lugging a water bucket to and from a pump a short distance up the street from the shop. This was for the men who were sweating away at the forges and shoeing the horses. At first I could only manage about half a bucket and the men weren't long emptying it with the dipper they shared. As I got used to it and could carry full buckets, my trips were less frequent and I had time to help in other ways. Little things, really, like bringing the men's lunches from Meg's kitchen out to the shop when they stopped work for a few minutes around noon. The four helpers boarded with the Dexters. And the lunches were always the same: large slices of bread with drippings on them and lots and lots of salt. The way they sweated, they needed that salt.

The Secret of the Spring

"On Saturday afternoons I had to go further down the block with my bucket, to a tavern. Instead of water, I would get a bucket of beer for the men so they could have a drink to celebrate the end of their work week.

"It was after one of these trips to the tavern that I found out what kind of a man Lloyd really was. I had been hurrying back to the shop with the foamy beer sloshing around in the bucket when the toe of my boot struck an irregular cobblestone and I tripped. Before I could recover, half the beer spilled out and ran down the gutter.

"I was crying and barely able to speak when I got back to the smithy and displayed what was left of the beer. When I explained what had happened, Lloyd winked at the men and said, 'Sure, sure, we've heard that one before. But for a little fella you sure can hold your booze.'

"They all had a good laugh as they shared what was left of the beer. Then Lloyd sent me back for another bucket and they all had extra rations that week.

"They were the good years, the best years of my life. The Dexters treated me as if I truly was their son. Lloyd was a great man. He taught me everything I needed to know. He was kind and gentle, but stern when he had to be. Meg had been a schoolteacher before they married and she loved to read, when she could find time. She was cooking and cleaning for the boarders and for ourselves, but she had her nose in every book she could get her hands on.

"I hadn't been with them more than a couple of days before she had me at my letters. Every evening, once supper was over with and she'd finished the dishes and swept up for the night, she would pull a book down from the shelf and read a chapter or two to all of us. Lloyd's helpers enjoyed this treat so much that they were always ready with the broom and dish towels, helping Meg with her nightly chores, eager to find out what was going to happen next in the book she was reading. I think one of her proudest moments came after I had been with them for a few years and she asked me to spell her off with the reading.

"It was almost like a competition between Lloyd and Meg to see who could teach me the most, and I was like a sponge absorbing everything and enjoying every minute of it.

"They would have sent me to school but there was no point. By the time I was twelve I was reading and writing and helping with the smithy's account books; a school would have done me no good.

"Lloyd's shop was successful because of the excellent service he provided his customers. He shod countless dray and coach horses but, unlike his competitors, he'd gained the business of the elite Londoners who kept stables on the Mall. In previous years these clients had had to send their horses to the blacksmith shops in the area and have their servants and hostlers wait, sometimes for hours, before their horses were ready. Lloyd attracted the lion's share of that business by offering a valet service. He would schedule the horses and have one of his helpers pick up the horses from the great houses and drop them off again when the work was done.

"By the time I was ten years old that became my job. From then on I spent hours in the saddle, or bareback astride carriage horses, running them back and forth from the smithy. I think that's when I started to develop these bowlegs of mine! On any given day you would see me flying through Rotten Row on some of the fanciest horses money could buy.

"But the shop wasn't all about shoeing horses. We also turned out some of the best wrought ironwork in the city. Lloyd had men working for him who could create beautiful spear-top fences and ornate gates. One of the men could craft iron flowers that looked so real you felt like watering them. I used to watch him work and he tried to teach me how to do it, but I never could. Some things can't be learned—they're a gift.

"One of the things Lloyd helped me with turned out to be more of a curse than a blessing, although his intentions were good. When I was about fifteen, I caught the eye of a young lass who lived some distance from the smithy. I used to see her when I was passing by on one of our customers' horses. After several chance encounters, I worked up the courage to stop and talk to her.

"We hit it off right away. She liked horses and I liked her. Whenever I met her, I would pull up and chat with her while she patted the horse's muzzle and asked me questions. After a while I felt more confident and would dismount and prolong our conversations.

"Finally I decided to put her to the test and see if the attraction was strictly horses. I asked her to walk out with me after church on Sunday. She agreed, so I told Meg about it and she made sure I was wearing my finest duds when Sunday rolled around. I met her and we spent the afternoon strolling along the Mall and talking, and not just about horses. It was a wonderful time and when I took her to her doorstep at the end of the day she even leaned over and kissed my cheek.

"I was happy as hell and walking on air when I headed for home, but I'd only turned the first corner when all that changed. Two large boys stepped out of an alley and blocked my way. One of the boys turned out to be the girl's brother and the other was someone who felt he had prior claim to her. What happened next was not pleasant.

"I wasn't a pretty sight when I staggered into our dooryard that night. Meg was going to have a lot of mending to do, and everybody present debated about whether it would take a doctor to straighten my broken nose. Even now it still wiggles around a bit.

"The very next night Lloyd escorted me to a tavern, where we met a man he knew. Jack was a burly old guy with cauliflower ears and puffy, slitted eyes. He'd been a prizefighter and was still agile and as strong as an ox.

"Over the next few months he taught me how to

use my fists and, to my disgrace, I became very good with them. Too good, it turned out. We were at it almost every evening for a long while. The old fighter had become a cab driver when he retired from the ring, and while he taught me, Lloyd shod his horse free of charge in exchange. It was a good deal for Jack because no horses in the city wore their shoes out faster than those who hurried hansom cabs over the rough cobblestones."

18: Don't you dare stop there!

"My first order of business after these lessons began to take effect," Ben said, "was to redeem myself in the eyes of my ladylove. I didn't manage that until about a year later. I found the boys who had beat me up and showed them what I had learned. I got each of them when they were on their own and found I could handle them with no trouble at all. Jack hadn't been putting me on when he said I had the knack. I was quick, and my work at the forge had made me strong.

The trouble was that once I got started fighting, something would come over me; I saw red and lost control. I know I inflicted more pain on those guys than was necessary, but I couldn't help it. That's my problem: I have a devil inside me that won't let me stop once my blood is up."

He noticed Lilly staring at his hands, and slipped them off the table into his lap.

"Those weren't the only fights I had. Word got out and, by the time I was sixteen, every young tough in the city wanted a crack at me. I'm not bragging, because I'm ashamed of it, but all the fights finished the same way, with my opponent badly beaten and the men who had come to bet on the fight dragging me off him. I'm telling you this now, lass, because I want you to understand about something that happened recently and I want the words to come from my lips before someone else tells you."

Her voice was very small. "Did you fight someone?"

"When I went to see your father and brothers that time, I'm afraid I lost my temper and maybe roughed them up a bit. It's not the first time your father and I have run rough against each other. There's bound to be bad blood between us now, and I don't think it will ever change."

Ben looked to Lilly for a reaction but she just sat expressionless, still looking at where his hands had been. He reached for the book they'd been reading and opened it to where they had left off the last time. "I suppose you've heard more than enough about my past life now, Lilly, so maybe we should stick to reading books."

"Don't you dare stop there, Ben Johnson!" Lilly exclaimed.

He had only been teasing her, but her reaction made him feel warm inside in a good way, so he put the marker back in the book, laid it down and continued with his own tale.

"Lloyd knew about the fights, but he just turned a blind eye. He never saw any of them but I always came home with some evidence of my opponents' efforts on my face. Meg would have known, also, but they never said anything to me about it. I don't know, maybe they were even secretly a bit proud.

Garry Leeson

"But when I was barely seventeen, it was one of those fights that changed my life forever."

19: Just trying to hide

"As I left the forge one evening," Ben said, "a man I didn't know approached me. He was a wizened little guy in a bowler hat who chattered away a mile a minute. The long and short of it was that a fellow was looking to test my skills, but it was not to be an encounter in the park or an alley. The man told me he had a barn where he staged fights and charged admission. He reasoned that since I was bound to tangle with the fellow in question at some time or another, I might as well get a few quid for my trouble. I guess I was flattered or just plain stupid, because I agreed.

"When I got to the barn the next night and pushed my way through the crowd to where they had a ring roped off, what I saw made me feel like turning around and running for home. In the far corner of the ring, with his back to me, a huge man in a military uniform stood stretching and flexing his muscles. When he turned around and stripped off his tunic, I realized I had been tricked—this was no boy and this was not his first fight. He was a man of about thirty, with a flat nose, tattered ears and more scar tissue than hair on his eyebrows.

"I looked around the crowd for the man who had duped me, but he was nowhere to be seen. I recognized several of the young men I had bested in the past clinging to the ropes and leering at me. I should have run but some kind of stupid pride made me stay."

Ben shook his head at the memory. "It was terrible. The man knew every trick in the book. Even though I tried to keep dancing away from him, he hammered me like no one ever had. I was all but beaten when, as it always did, the madness came over me and nothing the big man could do would stop me. I punched and kicked and even bit. Everything became a mad whirl and continued until I felt them dragging me off him and I heard someone say that I had killed the man.

"I got to my feet, grabbed my shirt and the crowd parted as I headed for the door. When I got home I had no choice but to tell Lloyd and Meg what had happened and they did what they thought was best for me.

"Meg packed a bag for me and Lloyd filled my hand with all the ready cash he had. With tears in their eyes, the pair of them sent me away, telling me never to return."

"And you just...left?" Lilly asked.

"I did, and I never saw them together again. I was tempted to write to them over the years, but I didn't want to take the chance that the law would find out where I was. I can still remember the night I left as clearly as if it had happened last week. Lloyd offered me the horse we kept in a stable at the rear of the smithy, but I said no. I didn't want to deprive them. Anyhow, I figured I'd be less conspicuous on foot at that time of night.

"Big Ben was booming the twelve strokes of midnight as I made my way through the east end out of the city, with all my worldly goods slung in a sack over my shoulder. I walked all night and the better part of the next day before I thought it was safe enough to stop and rest. And even then, I didn't want to chance an inn. I bought my food in the villages I passed through and slept anywhere I could find a bit of shelter.

"Coaches were always overtaking me as I trudged along. When they did, I ducked into the hedges until they passed. I knew they might be carrying the news of what I had done.

"I wandered for a long time, always heading north.:

"Why did you choose north?"

"I had no good reason, but somehow I figured that Scotland might be a good place to hide." Ben smiled shyly. "I was just trying to hide, like an animal. I didn't really have a plan.

"About a week later, I happened on a huge haystack in a field by the road. It was around dusk and the gate was open, so I went to the far side of the stack and burrowed into it for the night. I was exhausted and fell asleep immediately. I dreamt that the man who organized the fight had gone to the Old Bailey and explained that the fight had been fair and that it was not my fault that the man died, and that I was exonerated.

"A rat ran over my chest and woke me up and I realized it had been a dream and that, in all probability, everyone involved the night of the fight was busy making sure I took the full blame, painting me as a murderer. I lay awake for quite a while, wondering what I was going to do. I tried to eat, but I had no appetite, so I tossed the food aside. It wasn't long before half dozen rats showed up to enjoy the baker's cooking even if I didn't.

"I was watching them fight over the morsels when I heard the sound of hoof beats pounding up the road. A horse was coming and it was coming fast. There was the sound of gravel flying as the horse came to a stop before turning into the gate in front of my refuge. I imagined it was someone who had been sent in pursuit of me and I sat tensed and waiting for him to come around my side of the mound. I decided that when he did, I wouldn't resist—I had done enough damage in the last few days. Lloyd and Meg would just have to watch me swing; I wasn't going to run any more.

"But nothing happened. So I decided it would be best if I just went around and surrendered. I got up, abandoned my bundle, raised my hands above my head and started walking slowly around to the other

The Secret of the Spring

side. I think I was mumbling "don't shoot" or something, I can't remember."

"Did he shoot at you?"

Ben shook his head. "When I got there all that I saw was a beautiful big black horse in full cavalry tack, munching away at the hay. He was on his own; there was no rider to be seen. After I made sure it was just the two of us, I approached him carefully and got hold of a broken set of reins that were hanging from his bridle. I ran my hands over the horse's neck and chest – he was hot and sweaty. He had obviously been running for a long while.

"I led him around to where I had left my things and he stood quietly while I fixed my sack to the back of the saddle. I decided that, after I let him rest for a while, I would get on him and put as much distance between me and London as I could."

Lilly's eyes were wide. "But that would be horse stealing."

"I know. But if they caught me, they could only hang me once, for the murder, so it was 'in for a penny, in for a pound'. I climbed into the saddle and headed up the road.

"I came to a milestone with a wooden sign shaped like an arrow. It was pointing north and said, 'Leeds'. I let the horse amble along for a while, but after about an hour I put him into a trot and he was content to keep up that pace for the next hour.

"I reined him in at the base of a steep hill and was thinking of getting down and walking him for a bit when his ears perked up and he started to whinny.

Then I heard it: the sound of hundreds of hooves pounding along the road ahead of us.

"I wheeled the horse around and looked for a place to hide, but for the last few miles I had been passing through a corridor of tight hedges with nowhere to slip off the road. I figured there might be a suitable spot over the hill I was climbing, and if I could get there before I was spotted, I might still have a chance to get off the road. I put the horse into a full gallop and headed up the hill.

"When I got to the top I realized that the terrain had played tricks with the sound: whatever was coming at me was closer than it had first seemed. I saw the tops of their lances first, and then the troop of cavalry appeared over a knoll a short distance away.

"I could have wheeled around and made a run for it but when I saw them break into a trot and head for me, I knew it was pointless. Their mounts were fresh and my guy was all but spent, so for a second time, I decided to surrender.

"My horse was eager to join up with those in the troop so I just gave him his head and let him jog toward them. As we converged with the troop they and I both slowed down until we came to a stop with my borrowed horse nose to nose with the pair in the first half section of the column.

"I was about to drop my reins and raise my hands when I heard someone say, 'Thank God you found him, lad. We have been tracking the Colonel's horse for two days now.'

"It was a sergeant. He dismounted, came over and gave the horse a quick inspection before turning to the front ranks and telling them that he was all right. Then he looked at my bundle, strapped to the saddle, and said, 'You must be one of the recruits the men signed up in Manchester last week. We were told to expect a few of you boys over the next few days. Climb down off there. It will be better if the Colonel sees me riding in on his horse. Take that colt I've been riding. He's a little frisky, so it'll give me a chance to see what you're made of.'

"I said nothing and just went along with whatever he said.

"When we arrived at Woolwich—that's the home base of the 17th Lancers—they turned me over to the Quartermaster. He asked me my name and scanned down a list of recent volunteers. When he didn't find it, I thought the jig was up, but he wasn't deterred.

"He just said, 'Oh what the hell, the more the merrier,' and added my name at the bottom. He gave me a uniform and a bunk in a barracks that was reserved for new recruits.

"A couple of them had already arrived, and over the next few days all the bunk beds filled up. Then we started our training.

"For the first two weeks all we did was march around on foot and drill back and forth in the horse paddocks. We might have made it through that portion of the training more quickly if some of the bumpkins in the class had known their right foot from their left. The sergeant finally had to resort to putting a piece of straw in the laces of the left foot of some of those idiot boys and so instead of saying, 'By the left quick march,' he'd say, 'By the straw foot, quick march!'

"I saw the last of that batch of boys when we headed to the stables and started learning how to ride and handle the horses. By then, everyone was aware that I knew my way around a horse, so I went directly into the regular troop and trained with them. The recruits I'd mustered in with were still trying to learn how to stay in the saddle when we got word that the regiment was going to ship out. They stayed behind, but I went. And that's how I became a Trooper and eventually a Sergeant in the regiment."

Ben stopped talking suddenly. He sat quietly for a few minutes and then, with his head hanging, he turned to Lilly. "Do you mind if we stop for a while?"

"Are you all right, Ben?" she said, touching his shoulder.

"Yes, lass. It's just that I haven't thought about those days for a long time and it's brought back some bad memories."

He patted her hand fondly. "We'll finish the story tomorrow night, if that's all right with you."

20: Half a league onward

The next evening Ben began, "In the early days of 1853, Britain, France and Turkey had got themselves into a scrap with Russia over a piece of land I had never heard of, and they sent us to straighten things out."

This evening, in addition to the atlas, Ben had taken a book of poems from the shelf and placed it on the table. "Before we get started, Lil, I want you to read this poem to yourself," he said, opening the book to a page he had marked.

"Don't you want me to read it out loud?" she said with a confused look on her face.

"No, I don't," Ben said firmly. "I've read it once and I'll never hear it again."

Ben went to the stove and topped up his coffee cup while Lilly read on—sounding the words silently to herself.

> Half a league, half a league onward
> > Half a league onward
> All in the valley of death
> > Rode the six hundred

As Lilly worked her way through the stanzas, Ben paced the floor. When she finally looked up at him, expecting him to be pleased with her achievement, he was still frowning and she was confused.

He came over and sat down beside her,. "Do you understand what you just read?"

"Except for a...'league'. How long is that?"

"Oh!" he said. "That's an old way of saying about three miles. So 'half a league' would be...?"

There was a long pause. Then she said, "A mile and a half?"

"Just the thing." He gave a flicker of a smile, then leaned forward. She nodded, still wondering what was troubling him.

"That poem is called 'The Charge of The Light Brigade' and it's a load of nonsense. I know because I was there. There was nothing gallant, brave or wonderful about it. It was called the Battle of Balaclava and the 17th was part of the Light Brigade. Pass me the atlas and I'll show you where we were."

With deep sadness etched across his face, Ben pointed out the location, then continued, "I hadn't been with the regiment long, but I had made quite a few friends. And I lost them all that day."

21: Rough shod

Lilly had never seen Ben's face so dark. He spoke to her, but his eyes looked right through her to some other place. She shivered.

"Those fool generals sent one hundred and forty-five of us Lancers and the rest of the regiments charging against the Russian cannons. When we finished, not really accomplishing anything, there were only thirty-eight of us Lancers left. That poem was just an attempt to glorify what happened that day. There was no glory and we weren't brave. Once we got started, we couldn't stop. If we had tried, the horses wouldn't have allowed it—they were more terrified than we were and had the bits in their teeth and were uncontrollable. It was insane, lances and sabres against ball and grapeshot, horses and men disintegrating in clouds of blood and guts.

"We didn't stop to congratulate ourselves afterwards; we were too busy cleaning up the battlefield. I was working with the Farrier contingent because, a couple of days before the battle I'd seen them falling behind their task of changing the horses' everyday shoes for heavier lethal shoes with battle caulks, and like a fool, I offered to help. We called it being 'rough shod'. The shoes became weapons that could do more harm to the enemy than our lances.

"After the stretcher-bearers carried the wounded and dead off the field, it was our turn. I now was considered part of the Farriers and had to help save what injured horses we could, and put the ones we couldn't out of their misery. We also had to retrieve the saddles and bridles and assist the Pioneers as they lopped one hoof off each horse. All the cavalry mounts had a registration number branded into one hoof and we gathered those hooves up after an engagement and gave them to the Quartermaster so he could keep a tally of the animals lost. In the interest of economy, we even had to go out and remove the shoes from the dead horses. It was awful to see those beautiful beasts reduced to stiff, stinking carcasses, staring up at you with glassy eyes and mouths contorted into horrible death grimaces."

He gave himself a bit of a shake and seemed to return to the room. "You know, maybe I should stop telling you these tales, Lil. I don't mean to upset you what with the little one coming along and all."

The look they exchanged confirmed that they both knew the stories would continue. Lilly wanted to hear them and Ben needed to tell them.

22: To do whatever he had to

The late summer days progressed into fall, and the mountain backdrop behind the forge and its companion buildings changed from various shades of green to a patchwork quilt of crimson and gold. Ben and Lilly continued in the routine they had established: working together at her lessons, discussing the books they were enjoying, but avoiding the obvious.

It was as if they were on an island together; and, in many respects, the little acreage was an island. A tall, bushy spruce hedge stood like a huge wedge around the perimeter of the corner property, obscuring any view from the road. The shop and barn filled the only gap. Lilly could go about her chores unobserved.

There was one window at the rear of the forge where it was possible for Ben's customers to see inside their sanctuary, but when he noticed some men sidling over in that direction, he decided to allow the soot from the coal he burned to accumulate on the panes until it was impossible to see through them. Except for the occasional visit from members of the Neilly family next door, the world left Lilly and Ben to themselves.

They were safe in their little world, but, as Lilly's

pregnancy blossomed and her stomach grew, Ben finally realized that they could no longer talk around the subject. They had to face reality and plan for the future.

Mrs. Neilly, who was the local midwife, had already volunteered to assist with the birth and come over to help them. However, it wasn't that aspect of the situation that troubled Ben. He was worried for Lilly's sake, but something he dared not put into words was troubling him more.

He knew about inbreeding. He had seen the results of it in the corners of the world his military career had taken him to and he had also seen the resulting aberrations right here in the Valley and on the mountain. He'd seen the misshapen children in the bazaars of Delhi—discarded children purposely disfigured further to enhance their capabilities as beggars.

He thought back to the day, just after he had taken over the shop, when one of the farmers off the mountain had approached him discretely to ask him to fashion a leg iron and a length of chain to, as the man put it, "Hold my son in the attic. He keeps chewing through the rope we use to tether him."

Lilly's child might avoid some of the worst possibilities and achieve an intellectual level similar to that of the girl's brothers, but there was always the possibility that Mother Nature would choose to show further displeasure. He tried to appear cheery and positive around Lilly as she started displaying her nesting instincts, fussing around the house and whatnot, but secretly his worries constantly haunted him.

One night he woke from a nightmare. He had dreamt that he came into Lilly's room and found her suckling a hideous little monster child.

That was when a dark notion began to take shape. He knew that he could not allow that to happen. Lilly, like it or not, had become his responsibility and he would do whatever was necessary to protect her from any further suffering.

He had moved from the barn to the daybed in the kitchen as her time drew near, to be sure to hear her when she needed him. He woke to the sound of her moving around on the floor above him. It sounded to him like she was getting out of her bed and shuffling back and forth across the room, then returning and plopping down for a short time before repeating the procedure.

He listened for a while, and when the unfamiliar noises above him continued, he threw off the bedcovers and reached for his trousers. The clock on the shelf was just striking three in the morning. He fumbled around on the top of the warming oven of the old wood range until he located the box of wooden matches, struck one and used its light to guide him to the table where the oil lamp sat.

He was nervous and the first match scorched his fingers and went out before he got the glass chimney off. He had to feel his way back to the stove and repeat the procedure a few times before he got the lamp lit.

When he eventually made his way across the kitchen and started up the stairs, he heard Lilly moan and he knew the dreaded moment had arrived. He spoke to her briefly through the closed bedroom door, trying to comfort her, telling her that he would fetch Mrs. Neilly as fast as he could.

He had kept the horse in the stable for the last two weeks in anticipation. He could probably reach the Neillys' house faster if he ran himself, but he knew it would take forever for Mrs. Neilly to navigate the dark road for the return trip, so he took the extra minutes to hitch his horse to the buggy.

Once on the road he wasted no time touching the old horse with the whip and putting him into a canter. He swung into his neighbour's yard and brought his horse to a sliding halt before abandoning the reins and running up onto the front porch, banging on the door.

"Take it easy! You'll break the glass!" he heard someone shout.

A light appeared in an upstairs window. Shortly Mrs. Neilly, lamp in hand, descended the stairs to the front hall. Ben watched as she hurried in his direction—she had either dressed very quickly or slept in her clothes, because she was ready to go with all but her coat, which she grabbed from a hook on the wall. She swung the door open and bent down to pick up her leather satchel that had been resting by it.

"I was expecting you yesterday," she said simply before allowing him to help her off the porch and into the buggy. As he clucked the horse into a trot

The Secret of the Spring

and then into a fast canter, she leaned into him and held onto his arm to steady herself.

Within minutes they were back in his dooryard and headed into the house. Ben abandoned the horse and buggy and followed Mrs. Neilly up the porch stairs, but she stopped him as she entered the house.

"You're not going to let that poor beast stand sweating in his harness all night, are you, Ben? You put him away and then come in and get the stove burning and boil me some water. I'll see to Lilly."

It was the longest night of his life. As a soldier campaigning in far-off lands he'd spent many a night waiting for battles he knew were about to start, but the tension he'd felt then paled before his present anxiety. He was worried to death about a girl he had come to love, but even more concerned about what kind of a child she was about to bring into the world.

He had made up his mind that he would not permit a life predestined to pain, suffering and abuse to go on any longer than necessary. He was prepared to do whatever he had to for Lilly's sake and, if he was honest, his own.

As the hours dragged on, he made several trips up and down the stairs with basins of water and the strips of linen Mrs. Neilly had assigned him to prepare to keep him busy. Between deliveries he tried to read by lamplight, but he couldn't concentrate. And it just wasn't the same without Lilly beside him.

At first there were only muffled sounds coming from above, but then he heard Mrs. Neilly shout, "For

God's sake, let it out, girl. If you feel like screaming, scream!"

Lilly was not long complying, and for the next six hours Ben was startled at regular intervals by bloodcurdling wails that had him wringing his hands and saying silent prayers.

Then, as he sat expecting yet another heartrending wail from above, he heard instead a single high pitched peep, followed by the sustained crying of a baby. He wanted to rush up the stairs, but restrained himself.

After what seemed like an eternity, Mrs. Neilly made her way down the stairs and into the kitchen. "Well, Ben, it looks like you got yourself a son."

Then after an embarrassed pause, she said, "I mean, Lilly's got herself a boy. The girl had a rough time of it and I gave her some laudanum just before I left her so she'll be drifting off to sleep shortly. You'll have to go up and see to the baby for a while. These old bones of mine won't stand much more, so I think I'll head home."

"Shall I get the buggy?"

"Bless you, no. You have a child to see to. Any road, the night air will do me good. That girl's roaring fair made my head split!"

Ben wanted to ask if the baby looked all right and normal, but he hesitated. If it turned out that there was a serious problem and he was forced to do what he felt was best for Lilly, the less said, the better. He was a brave man, but what he had decided he would

The Secret of the Spring

do if necessary took a different kind of courage, and he wasn't sure he would be up to it.

Ben stepped into the yard and made sure the water trough was full before he headed up the stairs. He pushed the bedroom door open and walked toward the bed.

Lilly was sound asleep with her baby cradled in one arm. Ben spoke to her softly but she didn't respond.

The baby was wrapped so tightly in a white cotton blanket that, in the sparse light that the lamp provided, he could see no part of the tiny body.

Ben reached down and gently lifted the child from her arms. Lilly didn't stir. He would examine the baby first, but if his fears were confirmed, he would take the deformed child to the yard, do what he had to do and stealthily return him to her arms. No one but he would know what he had done and he would take his secret to the grave.

He lost his resolve momentarily and let the tiny bundle rest back into the crook of Lilly's arm, but then he recalled the horrible dreams he'd been having and lifted the baby again.

He placed the baby near the foot of the bed, where the lamp light shone brightest, and started to unwrap him. Ben's big hands were not accustomed to the delicate task, and when the last fold finally peeled off and his calloused palm touched the baby's tender skin, the child let out a sharp cry and his eyes opened.

They were the biggest, bluest, most knowing eyes

he had ever seen and they stared directly at him. It was as if he knew what Ben was up to.

Ben avoided his gaze and started examining his body. To his surprise, everything seemed to be in order: no webbed toes, no hair lip, a beautifully formed head with a fuzz of golden hair and nothing, nothing visibly irregular.

He grasped the little naked body in both hands and raised him above his head where the light was better, and the baby gave another sharp cry and their eyes met again. It was as if the child was seeing right into his soul, and suddenly the big blacksmith broke into tears and cuddled him to his chest.

Lilly woke two hours later to the sound of her son's mewing. She sat up and looked around the room frantically, before spying Ben sitting in a rocker by the window. He had the baby in his arms, rocking ever so gently and talking to him.

When she saw him look over to her, she said quietly, "You two are the prettiest picture I ever saw."

Blushing, Ben got to his feet and carefully returned her baby to her. He turned his back as she slid the child under the sheet and offered him her breast for the first time.

23: Smitten

Ben had to admit it: he was smitten. All he could think about was Lilly and her beautiful boy child. Mrs. Neilly had made herself available to help out with mother and baby, but after three days she realized that the doting Ben had things well in hand, so she left their care to him.

Ben spent his days working sporadically in the smithy, but more often he tossed his apron aside and, after washing his hands in the water trough, eagerly ran up the stairs with food, cups of tea and clean diapers. Lilly wanted to be on her feet and back at her chores right away, but Ben insisted that she spend several days convalescing in her room.

They had agreed that the baby's name should be Daniel but instantly it became, and remained, Danny.

One evening Ben appeared in the room with the book they had been reading before the confinement. "I was thinking...I could continue reading to you from where we left off."

Lilly put him off, saying, "Please, Ben, not the book. Just keep telling me the story about what happened to you after Balaclava. Anyway, your stories are better than most of the ones we've been reading."

She settled little Danny's head so he was facing

Ben, mimicked a pouting child's voice and said, "And Danny wants to hear your stories as well."

Ben put the book down and sat on the corner of the bed. "Well, all right, if his nibs is interested, I guess we could yarn a bit."

"We're ready," Lilly said on Danny's behalf.

But Ben was on his feet again. "I better go down and get our atlas, so you can understand where we went to next."

He wasn't away long. He sat at the head of the bed beside her and opened the book at a double-paged map. Looking down at little Danny, he said, "Can you see this all right, young fella?"

Danny was looking in every direction except at the map, with intense interest.

24: The ever-present atlas

Ben said, "This would be in 1855, mind. Almost thirty years ago."

"Before I was anything," Lilly said with a small smile.

"Not even a twinkle in an eye. Well. When we were half-rested and ready, and the generals had no more use for us, we dragged ourselves back from the Crimean Peninsula, limped across Europe and loaded what were left of our horses on barges on the French side of the Channel. Old England never looked so good to me. I could have knelt and kissed the ground when we landed home.

"We slow-marched the horses back to Leeds and our station at Woolwich. When we arrived at the station, the place was abuzz with new recruits and troopers sequestered from other units to make up for our losses. The men who had signed up with me, but had been too green to take with us to the continent, were now wearing their spurs and strutting around like old veterans. We spent a couple of months recuperating and enjoying some time on leave in close-by Manchester and York.

"I was sorely tempted to contact Lloyd and Meg. I think I might have taken the chance if one morning we weren't called up to Headquarters and the Colonel announced that we were leaving for Ireland immediately.

"The Irish Sea was no calmer than the Channel had been, and most of us were seasick. The horses, crammed in narrow stalls below deck, suffered as much as we did. When we got ashore, the pleasure of setting foot on solid ground was only brief. We found out that our mission was a sort of police action to protect the interests of England in a country that for the most part despised us.

"We went from being cheered, as we rode through the streets of English towns, to being booed and spat at as we made our way cautiously through the streets of Ireland. We put up with it for the better part of two years, until something happened on the other side of the world that granted us a reprieve of sorts."

The ever-present atlas lay open on the bed and, after pausing to thumb through the pages, Ben stopped and pointed. "Do you see all those pink countries on the map, Lilly? Those are all part of the British Empire. They say it's so big that the sun never sets on it."

Lilly frowned. "But when do people sleep?"

Ben laughed. "No, no. I meant, no matter what time of day it is, there's some part of the Empire where it's daytime. See that patch right there? Well, that's India, and that's where we went from Ireland."

"And sometimes it would be day in India and night in Ireland?"

"Well, yes, I guess that's so."

The Secret of the Spring

"But why did you go to India? It's so far."

"A bunch of the Indian soldiers got mad because some silly bugger in England used pork fat to grease the bullets they were using. Eating pork is against their religion so it turned out to be a real problem. They mutinied—"

"They what?"

"It means they stopped obeying their orders. In fact, they started fighting against our army. They massacred British officers, enlisted men and the civilians that they had once served. The mutineers were called sepoys."

"That's a silly name for killers."

"Anyway," Ben said, "the government figured they could use our help, so we shipped out of Ireland as soon as we could. The thing is, the route we took was so damned long that by the time we got there, the situation had more or less been cleared up. I saw how they punished some of the more violent mutineers and it wasn't a pleasant sight."

"Wait," Lilly said. She put her hands gently over Danny's tiny ears. "Now say."

"They would strap a sepoy to the front of one of the cannons, and when the big guns fired, well, there wasn't much left of them for their families to bury."

Ben gazed down at Danny. "There I go again telling you two things I shouldn't. I'm sorry."

"Since you are here, I know you never die in any of these stories, so I can bear it. Tell us more."

"Ah. Well, we did see a little action there, and it could have ended ill for me. There was one rebel leader, a fellow called Tantia Topi, who was still at large. We spent months tracking him down before we finally caught him at a place called Mangrol. Our little troop had to charge into a group of five thousand native cavalry to get to him, but we pulled it off. They hanged the fellow shortly after.

"We spent eight long years in India, and oh, the tales I could tell you about that place. Someday I will, but not right now."

Lilly, with her little charge, was always tired. She was almost asleep before Ben could say goodnight.

25: You like to leave me hanging

Lilly woke from an after-supper nap to find Ben seated with Danny in the rocking chair by the window.

He looked over to her and said softly, "I was thinking about the time I saw the ghost."

Lilly smiled at him as if he was joking but he remained serious and continued rocking and quietly talking.

"It's true, girl, and it happened on the troop ship on the way home. This would be in 1865, like. Our horses stayed behind in India, so I had a lot of time on my hands and was able to mingle and play cards and toss dice with the men of the other regiments on board. Most of us took every opportunity to stroll the decks when the weather would permit.

"That's when I saw him. He was leaning on the rail, with the setting sun behind him making it hard to distinguish his features. With one arm in a sling, he was obviously one of the wounded they cared for in a hospital section below deck. I couldn't see him clearly but there was something about him that made me want to have a closer look. He wore a tunic with corporal stripes draped loosely over his shoulders, covering his bandaged right arm in its sling. I could see that he had a pipe clutched between the fingers of his good hand and as he heard me approach, he swung around and asked for a light.

"That's when I recognized the flat nose and mutilated ears and realized who he was. The man I thought I'd killed in the ring all those years ago was alive and standing in front of me.

"I was so shocked I couldn't speak. Do you realize what that meant, Lil? I had been running and hiding for all those years for no reason. It meant that I had left a happy home and broken the hearts of the only two people I loved. I knew that Lloyd had planned for me to take over his smithy when he retired, and if I had stayed, he would have been taking it easy by now and I would be in charge. If only I had contacted them when I was tempted to years ago, I would have found that out and been able to return home.

"All of these thoughts were rushing through my head before I spoke to the man, and he seemed confused by my silence. I helped him light his pipe before I explained who I was and even then, he didn't seem to recognize me.

"He said that he'd had hundreds of fights and been knocked unconscious in more than a few. He seemed to remember a bit about our match, but he certainly didn't attach the importance to it that I did.

"That was the only conversation I had with that man during the voyage home but, based on it, I prepared to make some big changes in my life. As soon as I got back to England, I would head for London and reunite with my family and see if they still wanted me to take over the business. If they did, I was eligible to muster out of the regiment within a few years and I would have no qualms about doing so; I would have done my time."

"Is that what you did, Ben?" Lilly asked.

"Ah Lil, the best laid plans of mice and men. Let's read some and I'll tell you what happened tomorrow."

"Darn you, Ben," she said with a smile. "I think you like to leave me hanging."

"Well then, Lil, maybe a bit more."

26: The Punch Bowl

Ben continued, "The rest of the voyage, which always seemed long, seemed even longer than usual. I paced the decks, rehearsing what I would say to Lloyd and Meg when I saw them. They had probably given up on me, thinking I was dead. It would be quite a shock for them, especially for Meg.

"I thought it might be better if I wrote to them first, but I knew I couldn't do that; I was too anxious to see them. We had been apart long enough. It had been over ten long years.

"Maybe when they heard what I had done with my life since I left in disgrace, they would forgive me. Maybe they would even be proud when I showed them my medals and told them how I had served my country.

"To my dismay, we were all ordered north back to Leeds without permission to leave, and it was almost a year before I was allowed an extended leave to go back south to London. Once I was given the go ahead, I grabbed my kit bag and got on the first train available. It had barely come to a stop before I leapt out and made my way to find a cab.

"The streets were so crowded that cab traffic was at a standstill, cabbies taking advantage of the lulls

The Secret of the Spring

to put nosebags on their horses. It was faster to walk, so that's what I did.

"When I finally rounded a corner and saw the blacksmith shop in the distance, I was so excited and my heart was beating so fast it felt like it would burst out of my chest. I avoided the shop and went directly to the front door of the house. I gave the old familiar knock I had used as child and then stepped back so Meg would appreciate the full effect of my dress uniform when she opened the door.

"I stood waiting for a response for quite a while and, when none came, I repeated my special knock, this time louder. There was still no response, and I was about to give it a third try when someone standing across the lane in the shop doorway hailed me.

"It was a man I knew from the old days, and when I went over to him, he gave me news I didn't want to hear. He took off his hat and mopped his brow and told me that Lloyd had died a few years after I left. He had cut his hand while trimming a horse and contracted tetanus. He said he was in horrible pain for the longest time, and his death had been a blessing. Meg had been with him the whole time and never let her emotions get the best of her until he was gone.

"She knew she couldn't keep the business going herself, but it was thriving, so there were plenty of takers waiting to get their hands on it. She bided her time and finally sold out to the highest bidder.

"Meg was from Yorkshire and, after Lloyd's death, she felt she had to go home. She wrote the fellow a letter after she was settled, telling him she had purchased an inn to keep her busy. If he remembered properly, it was called The Punch Bowl and was on the moors somewhere in an area called Swaledale.

"I knew the place. It wasn't but a day's ride from the depot at Leeds! To think we had been that close to each other for all these years..." Ben shook his head. "I went to the cemetery where the man said Lloyd, my only true father, was buried. I said my goodbyes to him before taking the train back north to Leeds.

"When I got back to the depot, I asked the Colonel for yet another leave for a couple of days. I told my story and the Colonel turned a blind eye while I borrowed a horse and rode north to find my mother.

"As I rode up the narrow lane leading to the inn, scattering a flock of sheep grazing on the verges, I saw her standing in the doorway. I was still some distance away when she turned toward me.

"She started down the stairs and closed the distance between us. When she was sure it was me that she saw, she whispered my name and waited until I flung myself out of the saddle and ran to her arms. We held each other for the longest time and for a moment I was that little orphan boy on her doorstep again."

He paused for a bit.

Lilly said, "I am trying to think of you as a little orphan boy. It's hard to imagine."

Ben spread his arms as if he, too, were amazed at what he had become. "I stayed with her for a week, longer than I had told the Colonel I would be, but we had so much catching up to do that I felt I couldn't leave. She wanted me to come and live with her and help with the inn. There was even a nice stone building on the property that would have suited perfectly for a smithy if I wanted.

"When we parted I told her that I still had obligations with the regiment, but when I could get clear, I would come and join her. Until then we would write each other and I would visit in my free time.

"I visited Meg as often as I could and did some smithing and the odd repairs whenever I was free to go. I loved being with Meg and helping her, but to be honest, I didn't feel as at home in the dales as I did in the regiment. My heart just wasn't really in it. I enjoyed the camaraderie and respect of the men in the regiment, and my role as a smithy and trainer there seemed more important than being an innkeeper.

"I wasn't too far from Meg and, because we seemed to be in peacetime, I could go to her whenever necessary.

However, things were brewing far away in the colonies."

"Which colonies?"

Ben smiled. "You remember that story, Lil, about the place where I got your ring?"

Garry Leeson

27: Close, but just not right

1890

Lilly was up and around now and, despite Ben's constant reprimands for doing too much around the house, things were getting back to normal. After supper, when baby Danny was down for the night and the day's work was finished, Ben and Lilly resumed their custom of reading before bedtime. Often now, Lilly would haltingly read a few passages, although her greatest pleasure was listening to Ben tell his stories.

One evening he took up from where he had left off some days earlier.

"It's hard to explain, Lil. Even though so much of what I saw as I travelled the world with the regiment was horrific, I still found myself longing for travel with my comrades and the excitement of battle. It had become an addiction. I felt I was wasting the best years of my life in those long, boring years that followed my return from India. I had long since become eligible to muster out of the 17th, but I couldn't bring myself to do it and I didn't have the courage to tell Meg. The tedium of running the smithy amid the dreary moors and the endless drills and mock manoeuvres that filled our time at the Woolwich depot seemed pointless."

"But the smithy was what you thought you wanted."

Ben raised his hands a few inches apart from each other. "That far off from what I wanted, I guess. It was close, but just not right."

"What did you do?"

"I have to tell you, there was more dangerous ground to be found in the Inn in Swaledale than at the depot. Every time I was on furlough, helping Meg and working at the forge, Meg would have some local eligible woman seated at our table, flashing knowing glances in my direction. Meg may have had the best of intentions, but I couldn't help feeling that it was also her way of tethering me. For the most part, relying on my military training in evasive action, I could fend off these attempts. But it wasn't easy—when a Yorkshire spinster sets her sights on you, you better have a good pair of legs or a fast horse at your disposal."

"Aw, you poor man, it must have been awful, Ben!"

"It's not funny, Lil. These things are sent to try us. I was still a young man and *The Times* and *The Yorkshire Post* were full of tantalizing tales of conflicts in faraway places. God forgive me, but I was sorely disappointed when the American Civil War ended. I knew of several troopers, mostly Irish, who had opted to abandon Britain and join in the fray, and I had been seriously considering it myself. For most, it was simply the lure of adventure and it didn't seem to matter to them which side they chose to fight for."

"Which side would you have chosen to fight for, Ben?"

"Not that it matters now, Lil, but I would have offered myself to the Union Army. Did you know that hundreds of men from around here crossed the border and fought for the North? Mr. Watson was here just the other day to get his horse shod, and he showed me the cavalry saddle he brought back from his service with the New York Mounted Rifles. He said he used the three hundred dollars that he got volunteering in place of a Yank who didn't want to go, to put a down payment on his farm on the mountain."

"But he could have died."

"He could have, indeed. Anyway, I missed my chance, but that wasn't the end of my interest in getting over to America and seeing some action. After the war the Union Army turned their attention to controlling what they called 'hostile plains Indians'."

"Why were they hostile?"

Ben paused a moment. "I suppose I would have been, too, if people were trying to take my land away. But you know, I didn't think about it at the time. I had the idea of joining one of their regiments, but it lost its glitter when, thanks to the new telegraph cable, we got the news that a large part of their 7th Cavalry had been wiped out at a place called Little Big Horn."

"I'm glad you weren't there."

"It didn't really matter, because the sergeants'

mess was now buzzing with rumours of some new deployment for the regiment. It was a sad day when I went to see Meg and, cap in hand, explained that I would be shipping out and not likely to see her for some time."

"Where did you go?"

"We went south in a troop ship. There were endless days on the ship as we headed slowly down the west coast of Africa. I wrote a letter to Meg every day but had no opportunity to mail them until we reached Cape Town. Then there was the long slow trek up to Ulundi. We could go no faster than the spans of oxen that pulled our supply wagons."

"What did you see?"

"Clouds of dust, flies all around my eyes, and the back ends of the oxen," Ben said with a tight smile. "There's the idea of romance, and excitement, and victory, but, really, most of a soldier's day is just eating dust and doing chores." He shook his head, amused at himself. "We did our time in South Africa. I've told you all about this before. That's where I got wounded."

He fingered the scar hidden in the hair on the back of his head.

"I remember."

"Well, I hadn't received a letter from Meg for a long time and hadn't been in any condition to send her one. After I was wounded I spent months in hospitals and more months on the hospital ship returning to England, so I guess that was to be expected. I wasn't in touch with her, but she was constantly in my thoughts."

28: It can cure things

Ben said, "I kept thinking about Meg fussing around her inn in the peaceful moors of Yorkshire, looking forward to when her long-lost son would return to ease her burden and be with her again as she drifted into her twilight years. As I lay healing from my wound and realized how close to death I had been, I knew that I had tempted the Grim Reaper too many times—my days as an active soldier were over."

"I am glad of it," Lilly murmured.

"I planned to make my way to Leeds as soon as we hit dry land but as I was making my way down the gangplank at the Millwall dock in London, I took another dizzy spell and blacked out. When I came to this time, I was in St Thomas' Hospital. I had lost two days. I spent a month there and although I sent several letters north to Meg, I never received a reply and I was beginning to worry.

"By the time I was deemed ready for travel and light duty, and received my chit for a railway ticket to our base at Leeds, there was still no reply from Meg. I made up my mind that I would bypass the city and go straight to Richmond where I could get a coach that would take me directly to Swaledale. I had to know why I hadn't received word from her."

Lilly hugged herself as if she were cold. "This sounds like bad news."

"You tell true." Ben sighed. "I guess when I climbed down off the coach and made my way to the door of the inn I expected to see the Meg I knew as a child waiting to take me into her arms again, but that was not to be. Instead a stranger greeted me and, after he realized who I was, led me to a quiet area of the pub and confirmed my worst fears: dear old Meg had passed away a year previous."

"Oh, no."

"I was devastated. On her death bed, knowing that I would be returning, she left directions for the pub to be sold and the funds to await me with her lawyer in Kirby."

Lilly frowned. "She left you all her money? So she must have cared for you all along."

"I believe so. Any road, I extracted my inheritance from a reluctant lawyer who, I could tell, had had other plans for the sizable sum. Then I returned to the base. I was still having the odd dizzy spell so they put me in charge of overseeing the training of young farriers.

"It was an easy job and I was more or less content with my lot over the years that followed until the regiment was called to active duty again and started to ship out. I was like an old warhorse—I'd heard the bugle call and wanted to be in the charge. I requested active duty again but they told me I was needed in Leeds and no amount of badgering on my part was going to change their minds."

"Did you really want to go into all that again?"

Ben smiled. "When it's over, you mostly remember the good bits, the friendships, the victories. The rest you push down in the back of your mind."

"But you didn't go."

"And I'll tell you how that came to be. About a month after the main contingent left and the base had settled down into a quiet training facility, we had a visit from a group of officers and noncoms from the King's Canadian Hussars. They were taking advantage of the absence of the senior commanders of the 17th to poach some instructors for their training facility in Nova Scotia at a place called Camp Aldershot. After a couple of nights in the mess with two of their sergeants singing the praises of the camp and the Annapolis Valley, I was sold on the idea.

Lilly said, "I don't need the map book to find Aldershot."

"We could walk there, yes. Any road, I no longer felt the same attachment to the regiment, what with most of the fellows that I knew long gone, so I signed the papers and took my leave. Soon I was on a ship headed for Halifax. I was billeted below decks with the noncoms while the officers shared the fancy quarters above us with the man who was behind the recruiting campaign—Sir Frederick William Borden.

"He wasn't such a bad fella. I had one of my dizzy spells when we were two days out to sea and he even came to see me in the sick bay."

"Were you sick long?"

"Oh, no. And it was one of the smoothest ocean voyages I've ever had. It seemed to me like a good luck omen, an indication of a better life waiting for me in Nova Scotia.

"I disembarked in Halifax—ten years ago, or a bit more—and took the train down to the Valley here. Camp Aldershot was still at its old location in Auburn and the accommodations were a little rough, but I settled in and started my duties. It was difficult to make friends at first. The militia recruits were Valley men and they referred to me as someone 'come from away'."

"People around here can be some thick," Lilly said.

"It made me feel a bit lonely and depressed. I thought I'd take a look at some of the Valley, so I took a young horse I was training and headed up this way. I stayed on the main road, but when I got to Middleton, the big gelding I was on started to flag, so I swung him north along the town's Main Street and started to return to the camp along the road at the base of the mountain."

"Our road!"

"You know it. The horse was thirsty, and when I came to a brook I dismounted to see if I could get him some water. The banks either side of the bridge were too steep so I led him into a grove of pines beside the road where the access to the little stream was better.

"As soon as we hit the shade of the trees and the horse's hooves crunched on the fallen needles I saw movement a little further up the slope. Four women were scurrying away with jugs in their hands. I led the horse up the hill to where the women had been. There was a very deep hole where the water was flowing rapidly up and out of the ground.

"My horse bent one knee, dropped his head and went at it eagerly. I tried a little myself but I found it bitter. That was my first taste of the spring water."

"People say it can cure things."

"I know. But the only thing it cured me of was the army, because it was on that very ride back to the base that I found this property."

Garry Leeson

29: No life for a woman

"Why is it you never married?" Lilly asked.

She waited through a long silence for an answer until she realized what she had said. Then she blurted, "Until you and me, you know—!"

"Well, it's like this, girl," he replied. "I won't lie to you. I've been with all sorts of women and they were scattered half way across the globe. The thing is, those that I would have had on a permanent basis wouldn't have me, and those that would have had me, the devil himself wouldn't have! And I was never in one place long enough before I came here to even think about it too hard."

Now it was Lilly's turn to look hurt. He stared at her for a moment, puzzled, and then quickly qualified what he'd just said, "That's, of course, until I met you, Lil."

They stared at each other for a moment and then both of them began laughing until they were in tears.

When they finally stopped laughing, Ben said, "Seriously, Lil, being a soldier's wife is no life for a woman. It means waiting at home alone for months and sometimes years, never knowing if her husband is going to return. Being a camp follower or sharing a partitioned-off bunk in a barracks with about twenty other men is worse still."

"Did they really do that?" Lilly asked.

"They did indeed, lass, and the privilege of hanging blankets around your bunk for privacy was mostly restricted to married sergeants."

"You were a sergeant, weren't you, Ben?" she asked, cocking her head to one side.

"Yes, my dear," he replied, "but I never treated myself to that luxury."

Garry Leeson

30: Your migrating bird

As Ben made his way from the house to the shop he turned and scanned the wooded slopes of the mountain behind his pasture and hay fields. He had been expecting to see it for days and now it was there: a plume of smoke was drifting up through the tops of some ancient hemlocks that grew in a gully on his woodlot about halfway up the mountain.

It was that time of year again, and Alphonse Arseneau had taken up residence.

Ben remembered with a certain amount of shame the first year he had taken over the smithy. He had seen that smoke and lost his temper and stormed up the trail behind the house, prepared to evict a trespasser. When he arrived at the source of the smoke, he found a neat little campsite. A two-wheeled cart rested, shafts upright, nearby, and a diminutive black and white piebald draft horse was hobbled and grazing on the meadow grass. A man about his own age sat astride a worn carving bench in front of a large tent. There was a kettle hanging on an iron tripod over the fire and the large stones that circled the pit looked like they had been in place for years.

Ben was out of breath from his climb, and as he tried to speak, the fellow beat him to it, uttering one word. "Tea?"

The Secret of the Spring

Ben was dumbfounded and stood there mesmerized as the man got up, walked over to the fire and filled two chipped enamel mugs from the kettle. There was a half-finished ash axe handle on the carving bench and several more finished ones were leaning against a fallen log that served as a bench close to the fire pit.

That's when he remembered. Someone had said there would be a demand for axes, hammers, forks, peevees and the like, and that he could depend on the travelling tinker from the French Shore to supply the wooden handles. They didn't mention that his main supplier would be taking up temporary residence on his woodlot each year.

As he sat cooling his temper while sharing the man's tea that morning, it dawned on Ben what a good arrangement it was, and over the years it had become more than just a business arrangement. He and Alphonse had become friends, sharing the stories of their lives and going fishing and hunting together when they could find the time.

Ben returned to the kitchen door and leaned in to alert Lilly. "Alphonse is back."

"Your migrating bird," she said with a smile.

"He'll be around sometime soon with a bundle of tool handles, no doubt, and I didn't want him to startle you. Or the baby."

"We don't startle that easy, Ben."

He scratched his head. "I suppose. But I heard he's taken a wife, so there may be more company than you would be expecting."

163

Lily peered out the door past Ben, as if she could see through the trees to Alphonse's camp. "Now I am curious to see who married him."

Ben was glad she would be at ease with their sometime neighbour. The men in the area didn't like Alphonse, and he didn't like them.

A few years ago one of his customers had spotted Alphonse in the yard and had started to say, "I see that that drunken bastard is back again and—"

Ben, wielding his hammer and glaring, had said, "You're talking about a friend of mine."

Nothing more was said that day, but, as time went on, Ben realized that, outside the sanctuary of his land, the slander and hatred of Alphonse and all the travelling kind persisted and probably always would. Alphonse had confided in Ben that he did have a drinking problem and a tendency to get rowdy when the rum took effect, but he never touched the stuff when he was around the blacksmith so it was no concern of his.

The next morning, Alphonse did indeed arrive with his first load of handles. Ben was still having his breakfast, and Lilly was fussing with the baby at the far side of the room. Suddenly the door flew open and the big Frenchman filled the doorway and shouted his normal request: "Tea!"

The baby gave a yelp of surprise, and Lilly turned and scooped him up. "Now then, now then. It's just Mr. Alphonse."

"The boy gives off a good alarm," Ben said, "but don't pay him any mind."

The Secret of the Spring

Alphonse slipped out of his shoulder straps and let his pack slump to the porch floor before he entered the kitchen and took Ben's hand. Then he swung around and said, "Come in, girl, don't be shy."

A girl made her way through the doorway. Ben was immediately struck by how beautiful she was with her dark shiny hair, fine features and olive skin. His first unkind thought was, "What is she doing with an old ogre like Alphonse?"

She was carrying a pack as well and he wondered why she hadn't taken it off before she entered, but the reason soon became clear. She went over to Alphonse and swung around. She wasn't carrying handles—she had a cradle on her back and a fair-haired baby with very dark eyes was looking around, taking in the room, and smiling.

Ben exclaimed, "What have we got here?" He turned to Lilly and was surprised to see her pale and staring. He swung around again and saw that the girl was also still, as if with shock.

Then, almost as if they had rehearsed it, Lilly thrust Danny into Ben's arms at the same moment as the strange woman shrugged her cradle off into Alphonse's. Then Lilly rushed to the girl and threw her arms around her as if to squeeze the life out of her.

Ben and Alphonse, both at a loss, stared at each other as the girls sobbed and whispered to each other. Finally Lilly turned to Ben and said, "Ben, this is Angie. My friend Angie."

Over tea and biscuits, with interruptions to tend the children, and explosions of tears and laughter, the girls explained where and how they had met. But, in a compact sealed in a quick glance, they did not go into details of what happened at the hotel.

As soon as they could, they left Ben and Alphonse to "man talk" about the year's events and took their babies out onto the porch.

"Tell me everything," Lilly said.

"Alphonse and I are married—well, sort of. I went back to Bear River after the, you know, the hotel. When I got home they told me my mother had passed away a month earlier. They sent somebody to the hotel to tell me so I could attend the funeral. The boy said he gave the message to the manager who said he would pass it on. That Worthington never told me anything, and I guess you know why. I found out he hadn't been sending her the bottles of spa water he promised either. I took the water I had brought with me and poured it on her grave."

"I am so sorry," Lilly said.

Angie gave a little nod of acknowledgement. "Well, then. I was back with my family, but I still had this little problem here," she said, hugging her child. "My people are good about this kind of thing. Nobody spoke ill of me or blamed me and there were several young men who were more than willing to take up with me."

Lilly gave her a quizzical look that seemed to say, "So why old Alphonse?"

"Those young fellows were nice and a lot of fun to be with, but ever since I was a little girl I was fascinated by Alphonse. While other men were leaving our community, working as farm hands and taking jobs in town, Alphonse held to our traditional ways as much as he could. He had all the skills of the younger men but he took the time to sit with the older folks and listen to the old ways and, when it was possible, practice them. In my eyes, he always stood taller than the rest of the men and I think I was spoony on him since first I saw him."

She leaned in closer and spoke low. "He was married before and had two sons, but they grew up and wandered off somewhere. His wife died a while back, so he was on his own. When I told him I wanted to be with him, at first he just laughed and said, 'You should have drunk more of that spa water, girl. Your eyesight is going.'"

"But you didn't give up."

"I kept at him, and when I started to get really big and couldn't do things for myself, he was there to help me. And then more than help me. He loves little Tommy here like he was his own and, do you know what, Lilly? I recently found out that older men are much better at other things, too."

Lilly blushed, put her head down and pretended to be adjusting Danny, not wanting to address the subject.

"He has his demons, too," Angie said. "He didn't drink often, but when he did he became different—a dangerous man. It has only happened once since we've been together and when I threatened to leave him if it ever happened again, he promised it wouldn't."

Doing something she had learned during her time at the hotel, Angie rapped the chair with her knuckles, saying, "And, knock on wood, so far, he hasn't."

31: No end of soft moss

Angie's presence was a blessing to Lilly. Alphonse normally stayed three months in the area but, at Angie's insistence, their time in the area stretched out closer to six months.

While Alphonse worked at his wooden handles, Angie kept herself busy with a skill she had learned from her mother. She spent hours weaving baskets from the thin strips of ash Alphonse provided. She fashioned countless large apple-picking baskets, but also made beautifully-detailed smaller ones for use in the home. One day Lilly was reduced to tears when Angie arrived on her doorstep with a carved and woven cradle that she and Alphonse had made together for little Danny.

The girls spent as much time together as they could. Angie would work at her baskets on the porch and look after the babies while Lilly went about her chores in the house and garden.

But they didn't always agree on everything. Angie would just shake her head when she saw Lilly slaving over the washtub, washing countless diapers.

"It's no better than doing laundry at the hotel," Angie said. "Look, there's no end of soft moss to be had in the woods."

"I don't know," Lilly said. "I don't want to put bugs and who knows what next to his skin."

But one day Lilly saw the wisdom of it. Danny had been bothered by a persistent rash on his little bottom and she was desperate for a cure. She decided to take Angie's advice and tried substituting moss for the cloth diapers. Despite her misgivings, within three days Danny's rash had cleared up.

Lilly reverted to her cloth diapers once he was better, but whenever the need arose she didn't hesitate to return to the moss cure.

Ben could see that it worked, but he too had misgivings—social ones. Mrs. Neilly happened over one afternoon when the girls were on the veranda shelling peas together and the babes were in Danny's cradle. They were happily lying there without a stitch on and the cradle was lined with the moss.

Mrs. Neilly just gasped and, after a quick hello and goodbye, headed straight back for home, shaking her head in dismay.

32: Something stirred

1892

It was little Danny's third birthday and they were having a party. Alphonse, Angie and their son, Tommy, had come down from their camp on the mountain to join in the fun. Lilly and Angie were in the kitchen icing the cake that Lilly had baked for the occasion and Alphonse was sitting in a rocking chair by the stove offering some constructive criticism.

"Where is that Ben?" Lilly said, wiping her hands on her apron and heading toward the screen door. "I told him to quit and come in early so he could clean up before supper. That man never stops working."

Lilly stopped at the door and stood looking out into the yard. A smile slowly spread across her face. After a while she said, "Angie, you better come and see this."

Ben had spent the better part of the previous day constructing a sand box for Danny. He had had to go three miles down the road with the horse and dump cart to where he knew there was the right kind of clean sand.

Now Ben was on his knees, laughing and helping the two boys construct a castle. He was showing them how to pack the moist sand into a small pail, flip it over and lift it up to create a perfect tower. The boys had a go at it themselves, adding a finishing touch here and there. Ben wrapped them in his big arms and hugged them as they admired their work.

"That's quite the man you've got yourself, Lil," Angie said, returning to the table and leaving Lilly still staring out the door.

Something stirred in Lilly. What Angie had said was true. He was her man—not her friend, not her father, but her husband, her man. She had been playing the good daughter to him all this time, but she no longer felt like a daughter. She felt like a wife, with all that that implied.

Angie had been at Lilly constantly, telling her that she should start acting like a proper wife to Ben, using the example of the wonderful relationship she had with "her old man," Alphonse. Lilly had to admit that she had found herself blushing recently when she watched through the window when Ben stripped off his shirt and washed his chest and arms in the water trough by the shop. He was a handsome man, muscular and as strong as an ox. She even liked the way he smelled as they sat close together at the table reading in the evenings.

He loved her little Danny and she had come to realize that she loved him. Maybe he didn't feel the same way about her, but she decided there and then that she would find out.

In a quiet moment she took Angie aside and confided in her. She told her friend that she was going to tell Ben about the way she felt when they settled down in front of their book that evening.

But Angie had a better idea.

Danny had had a big day and Ben was required to tell three bedtime stories instead of the normal one before the child settled down and he and Lilly could kiss him goodnight.

"We've all had a busy day," Ben said quietly. "Maybe we should make it an early night and pick up the reading tomorrow."

"I suppose so," Lilly said.

In the kitchen, Ben lit his candle, leaned over and gave Lilly his customary peck on her forehead. "Goodnight, then."

He headed up the stairs to the third bedroom he'd recently started occupying instead of the daybed behind the cookstove. He set the candle on the bedside table, undressed and pulled on his flannel nightshirt over his head. Then he climbed into bed, leaned over and blew out the candle.

He was on the edge of sleep, reviewing the events of the wonderful day, when he heard footsteps in the hall and the hinges of his bedroom door creaking.

"Is that you, Lilly? Is there something wrong?"

She didn't answer. She just walked to the bed, climbed under the covers, snuggled up beside him and whispered, "I love you, Ben."

Ben wrestled with his emotions. It was the last thing he expected to happen. He and Lilly had had an unspoken arrangement. They had fallen into a routine that he assumed would continue until somebody more her age came on the scene and displaced him. He had only hoped that if and when that happened, Lilly, and whomever she chose to be with, would still allow him to be with Danny, maybe as a sort of a grandfather.

But God help him, as she pressed herself into him he didn't—couldn't—resist.

In the cold light of day the next morning, Ben felt terribly guilty. He let his work wait while he lingered in the kitchen to talk things out.

Lilly was buzzing around the kitchen doing her chores and humming a quiet tune, looking happy and content, while he sat at the table, seething inside while trying to smile and appear happy. He thought, *I'm no better than her brothers and father now.* He had taken advantage of her. He had done something that would cause him to lose her forever.

He loved her, of course. He always had, but not in that way. He thought those words, but he knew he was lying to himself. Maybe it had been true in the beginning, but as she had become a woman—a beautiful woman—he began to have thoughts and dreams about her that he was not proud of.

"Come sit with me a minute, lass," he said pulling out the chair beside him.

She was beaming as she sat down and looked up at him with a smile on her face.

He came straight to the point. "About last night, Lil, I'm sorry—I shouldn't have done that. It won't happen again. We'll have to find a place for you and Danny to live and—"

He stopped as he saw her eyes filling with tears.

"You don't want me?" she cried. She got to her

feet, turned from him and buried her face in her apron.

Ben leapt to his feet, spun her around and wrapped her in his arms. "For god's sake, girl, of course I want you. I want you with all my heart. But it's not right. I'm too old for you. You deserve better and I shouldn't have taken advantage of you.".

Ben let his arms drop to his side, but she clung to him and whispered into his chest, "You didn't take advantage of me, Ben. I took advantage of you. I loved every second of what we did. I'm not going anywhere. I'm your wife and you've made Danny your son, so you better get used to it."

"But Lord save me, Lil, when you're still a young woman, I'll be old and ready for the grave. What'll you do then?"

"I guess I'll cross that bridge when I come to it," she replied.

She took his hand and led him to the stairs, whispering, "C'mon. Danny's still asleep."

For the rest of their lives they never slept a night apart.

Life around the blacksmith shop at the base of the mountain took on a new meaning. Lilly stopped being the shy girl who hid in the house when strangers approached. She became proud of her status as the wife of such an intelligent, important, and worldly man. Ben ceased being the over protective father-figure and assumed the role of the proud husband of the prettiest woman in the Valley.

He no longer made the trips to town for supplies

on his own. His little family walked proudly through streets of Middleton—little Danny swinging along between them or riding on Ben's shoulders.

Their age difference ceased to be an issue as the years passed. Lilly, to her delight, became known as Mrs. Ben. There were still whispers about Lilly's past, but God help the man or woman who voiced them aloud in earshot of Ben.

33: No time for niceties

Ben was worried—something was very wrong with Danny. The boy woke up with a fever and swollen cheeks and didn't want to get out of bed.

Lilly prepared his favourite breakfast of eggs and bacon and brought it up to him on a tray, but the child just rolled away from her moaning, "My head and my ears hurt, Mommy! They really hurt, Daddy"

It was the word Daddy that did it.

It was the first time the boy had called him that, and Ben wasn't about to just stand there and watch his son suffer.

"Stay close to him, Lil. I'm going for the doctor."

Ben tore down the stairs and out the kitchen door, running right past a customer who was waiting to get a shoe replaced on his horse.

"You know where the tools are. Tack the shoe on yourself and come back later and I'll check it for you."

There were two horses in the stable. His old gelding, Charlie, stood snoozing in a stall. In the other stall a tall, dapple-grey thoroughbred stallion was tethered, waiting for his owner to pick him up. Ben had shod the horse with light racing shoes the day before.

He pulled his saddle and bridle off their rack and

headed over toward Charlie but stopped just before entering his stall. He took one look at the old horse and muttered, "To hell with you, you tired, old brute. I'm taking that stallion and I hope the owner won't mind."

Minutes later Ben was mounted and flying full tilt down the road.

Ben and Lilly, depending on the occasional ministering of Mrs. Neilly, had never felt the need of a real doctor. Although he had never met the man, Ben had heard good things about Doctor Rutledge in Middleton, and that was where he was headed.

Ten minutes later Ben brought the stud to a skidding halt in front of the doctor's house. He quickly dismounted and handed the reins to a large boy who was just emerging from the front door.

Pushing past him into the empty office, Ben shouted to no one in particular, "I'm Ben Johnson. I've got a very sick boy at home. I need you to come with me right away."

Presently a diminutive figure in a white coat emerged from a back doorway. The stature of the man seemed inconsistent with all the stories that Ben had heard about his exploits.

Jesus! The man can't weigh more than eight stone and looks shy of fourteen hands high.

Aloud, he said, "Are you Doctor Rutledge?"

"I am, sir. How can I be of assistance?"

"I've no time for niceties. I've got a very sick six-year-old boy with a high fever and swollen glands. I need you and I need you now!"

The look on Ben's face was the only incentive the doctor needed. Stripping off his lab coat, he grabbed his satchel and moved swiftly to the door and shouted to the waiting boy, "Tiny, hitch King to the buggy and be quick about it."

"*King?*" Ben moaned. "That's not King, the old Standardbred that used to belong to Eric Watson, is it?"

"It is indeed, and a good, dependable horse he is."

"Doctor Rutledge, do you ride?"

"The 13th Hussars seemed to think so, Mr. Johnson."

Ben grabbed him by the arm and dragged the little man, his bag in hand, out to where Tiny held the prancing stallion. "Let me give you a leg up and I'll hand you your bag."

Without a word of protest the doctor allowed Ben to almost fling him into the saddle.

"Wait, I'll adjust those stirrup leathers for you, Doc."

"Tell me where I am to go, as well."

"My soul, I am a fool" Ben said.

He quickly described the smithy, the house beside it, and the best route. "Lilly is my wife. Do you think you can find your way?"

For his answer, the doctor dug his heels in and sped off in the direction of the smithy.

Ben helped Tiny get King harnessed and into the shafts, but before getting in beside the boy, he gathered two big handfuls of small stones.

They set off with the Standardbred assuming his

regular leisurely pace, but Ben was soon pelting the horse's rump with the pebbles and getting the best out of him. The best was not much, however, and it seemed like an eternity until the smithy appeared in the distance.

The doctor had made good time, and when Ben had a view of his house, Doctor Rutledge was walking into the yard with a limp boy in his arms.

Oh, my God, I'm too late! I'm too late!

Ben watched as the doctor, followed closely by Lilly and recently-arrived Angie, made his way over to the water trough.

My God, what's he doing?

As Tiny reined King to a halt in the yard, a strange scene unfolded. Alphonse was standing off to the side holding the sweaty, spent stallion while the doctor, aided by Lilly and Angie, was involved in a strange baptism. They were gently lowering Danny into the trough with a sheet, letting the cool water wash over his feverish body.

As Ben rushed toward them, he was struck by the horrible memory of what he once had thought he might have had to use that trough for.

"It's all right, Ben," Lilly stammered through her tears. "The doctor knows what he is doing. We need to get his fever down."

Ben took a corner of the sheet and helped dip and lift the boy for the better part of half an hour. He barely noticed that the owner of the stallion was standing at a distance but watching intently.

Finally Danny began to complain and thrash

The Secret of the Spring

feebly, using some language he must have heard down at the smithy

"We have turned the corner," the doctor said. "Now we can return him to his bed."

Ben and Lilly stayed by Danny while Angie fussed around the kitchen, looking after Tommy. She quickly made some tea and ferreted out the oatmeal cookies that Lilly had stashed away in the larder.

Leaving further instructions and some medication to ward off the effects of what he diagnosed was a case of the mumps, Doctor Rutledge closed his bag and descended the stairs.

In the kitchen, Angie was standing ready with a mug and a plate.

"I thank you for the thought," the doctor said, "but I cannot pause."

He took a sip of tea and handed the mug back to her, then wrapped two of the cookies in a handkerchief which he slipped into his coat pocket. "I have other urgent business waiting for me in town, but these may sustain me through it."

A few minutes later, Ben glanced out the window of Danny's room. In the yard below he could see that the owner of the stallion, holding his horse's lead shank, was having what appeared to be a heated discussion with the doctor.

"I've got to get down there, Lil. There's trouble brewing and it's my entire fault. I should never have used that horse and I sure shouldn't have got the doctor involved."

Ben hurried down to the yard. By the time he got

there, the man was leading his stallion away and Doctor Rutledge had assumed his seat in the buggy beside Tiny.

"Hold on, Doctor, hold on. I've got to apologize to you."

"Whatever for?"

"That man, the owner of the thoroughbred. I could see that he was mad at you for using his horse, and that's my fault."

"Don't be so foolish. The man said he'd never seen his horse move as fast as he was going when I rode in. He was miffed when I told him I wouldn't jockey the animal in a race he's got scheduled for next week!"

34: A note of whimsy

While Danny made his slow recovery, Doctor Rutledge made daily visits, conveniently around dinner time. Lilly, under Mrs. Neilly's tutoring, had become quite a good cook and the doctor and Tiny looked forward to having their dinner with the little family at the big kitchen table, where the seeds of a friendship were being sown.

Ben really liked and respected the doctor and was impressed with the common-sense approach he used while plying his trade. It was a special kinship; they were both British expatriates trying to fit into a new home.

Although they never broached the subject again, the doctor had let slip that he had served with the 13th Hussars. It told Ben all he needed to know about the man's past. For those who had survived it, Balaclava was a word best left unspoken.

At one of their encounters out of Tiny's presence Doctor Rutledge explained a bit about his assistant and driver. "You know, I imagine, that many men in this area get nicknames pasted to them that defy the obvious."

"It puzzled me at first," Ben said. "I thought it might be because there are so few last names. I can think of six Thomas Smiths between here and Windsor."

The doctor nodded. "Sure, that plays into it. But there is a note of whimsy as well. As to Tiny, well, he is so tall and heavy-set that it seems a stubborn refusal to acknowledge the facts of his size."

"He does not seem to mind it."

"That is a mercy. His real name is George, did you know that?"

"I did not," Ben said.

"Imagine my confusion while trying to properly identify my patients," the doctor said. "Every man's true name is rendered redundant except on birth records and death certificates. I wonder what nickname they're going to paste on me…"

Ben, who had heard folks refer to the diminutive doctor as both Moose and Bull, held his peace.

35: Primum non nocere

There was bad blood between Dodger Duffy and Doctor Rutledge and everybody knew what had caused it. Ben had heard the story several times from various people and once directly from the horse's mouth.

One day, when he and the doctor were alone in Ben's smithy, Duffy's name came up. The doctor put up a warning hand, strolled to the front of the smithy to make sure there were no idle ears nearby, and then came back to stand close by Ben.

"I feel I should warn you about doing business with that Dodger," he said in a low voice. "Most of the people I treat are honest, hardworking folks who pay for my services, one way or another. I have a larder full of foodstuff that people have given me when they had no cash. But this Duffy fellow is a worthless scoundrel with no sense of honour."

Ben settled in and listened.

"One night, three winters ago, a galloping team of horses pulled up in our dooryard, shaking my household awake. As everybody knows, I never lock the door to the clinic, and soon someone had made his way in and was shouting up the stairwell to our bedroom. When I looked down from our window I could see a pair of horses hitched to a heavy bobsled standing untended. A cloud of steam hung above the animals and they appeared to be on their last legs.

"I threw on my clothes and went downstairs, to find Budgey Lewis, lord knows what his real name is, He's a slow-witted guy with a peculiar speech impediment."

"I know him," Ben said.

"Budgey was in such a state of excitement and distress that I could hardly understand him, but finally I thought I had it. It seemed that someone was very seriously injured up at a logging camp.

"You know that Budgey is prone to exaggeration. I had to take that into account when trying to fathom what the extent of the injury might be. In any event, I knew the logging boss at the camp wouldn't have sent him flying down South Mountain without good cause, so I got ready for another sleepless night. Tiny had anticipated trouble and was already in the stable harnessing King.

"I thought that if the road weren't too rough I would be able to catch some sleep as we slid along. It was lucky that Tiny knew where we were headed, because getting directions from Budgey would have taken the better part of the night. We left Budgey to return on his own, telling him to walk the tired team slowly. It was a rough trip but I did get a little sleep.

"When I got into the shanty, I found Duffy lying on his back on a blood-soaked blanket atop a makeshift pallet in front of a big old iron stove that was the only source of heat in the place. Several men were taking turns trying to stem the flow of blood from an ugly, foot-long gash in the victim's leg, apparently the result of an encounter with a carelessly-stored double-bitted axe.

"After a quick look at the wound I had the men lift Duffy onto a table in the mess hall. I had a complicated stitch-up job ahead of me and my patient was being uncooperative, to say the least. Dodger was full of piss and vinegar, swearing like a sailor. I was relieved when the chloroform kicked in.

"The procedure took more than an hour, and another hour for Dodger to come out of the anaesthetic. When he came to, I told him he needed to go to the hospital because his wound was very serious. If it got infected, he could lose his leg.

"Dodger said he wasn't going to any damned hospital, so I told the camp manager he'd better arrange to get him to his home in the valley, where his wife could look after him.

"We decided that a rough ride down the mountain on one of the company's bobsleds would probably pop out my stitches, so I decided that Tiny and I would see him safe to his home in our sleigh. The detour to Dodger's house added an additional hour to our trip home but, 'primum non nocere.'"

"Sorry, what?"

"Oh," the doctor said. "That means 'first, do no harm'. It's part of an ancient oath doctors take. So, you see, I had no choice."

Ben had known more than a few medical folk who had seemed to go out of their way to cause harm, but he held his peace.

"When we finally arrived at his house, Tiny and I managed to lug Dodger in and settle him on a cot behind the kitchen range. I knew I would have to make several return visits to monitor and treat the injury, and I wasn't looking forward to it. But somehow I made the time and saw him through the worst.

"When I finally went to remove the stitches and pronounce the wound healed, I noticed bruising on his wife's face. She claimed she had bumped into a door. That seems to happen a lot in houses in that neck of the woods."

Ben nodded. "Some men treat their oxen better than their wives or children."

"I spent a lot of time looking after that man, and had to decide how much I was going to bill him. They didn't have much to start with, and of course Dodger hadn't been working since the accident. I figured out the time and the cost of the medicine and chloroform, and cut the total in half. Bad business but good riddance.

"I sent the invoice by mail. And then I sent a reminder a month later...and every following month over a period that has stretched out to years now. The man has lots of money now, and is well able to pay, but he just flaunts my attempts to collect."

The doctor fetched his casebook from his coat pocket, and produce a much-folded sheet of paper from the back of the book. "I have been carrying this copy of that invoice around with me for years, and I have pushed it into his face when I have encountered him several times. He just makes a rude comment and walks away."

The doctor's mood darkened as he returned the invoice to his casebook. "I have recently learned that his poor wife met with an accidental death. A death that might not have happened if I had not struggled so hard to heal Dodger."

He shook his head slowly and muttered what sounded like a curse, but Ben couldn't quite make it out.

36: Paid in Full

Tiny Mosher came rushing into the crowded smithy with a bent horseshoe in his hand.

"The doc needs help, Ben. We've just come from Joe Martin's up on the mountain. The doc had to amputate his leg and he has been with him most of the night. When we got down here this morning we got word that there was an emergency up Paradise way that we had to get to. We was on our way and just down the road when King threw a shoe. The Doc's outside asleep in the buggy."

The men waiting at the smithy immediately cleared a path. As Ben headed for the door most of them nodded their approval, even though it meant waiting longer themselves.

There was only one dissenter.

"It's *his* emergency. Why should it cost *me* lost time?" Dodger Duffy said.

Ben hesitated, but so many words occurred to him to say in response that they all jumbled together before they could escape his mouth. He just gave Dodger a long look and continued outside.

Before long, the shoe was on the horse. He turned back toward the forge, only to find himself face to face with Dodger, who waved a bouquet of dollar bills in front of Ben's face. "You got time for the high

The Secret of the Spring

and mighty, but no time for us working folk. I guess poor people's money is no good here today!'

"I'll be glad to take it when it's your turn and I've done your job," Ben said.

Dodger started to stuff his money back into his purse. "It would be done by now, if you knew your business."

He gave Ben his shoulder, only to find himself facing the doctor, who was less than a pace away.

Dr. Rutledge opened his mouth to express his condolences over the loss of Dodger's wife, and to tell him to forget about the invoice that he had been carrying so long. But before he could speak, Dodger, cramming his money into his purse with one hand, shoved the doctor back with the other.

"I'm tired of you pestering me over that damned bill," he shouted. "Shove it up your arse. If you want payment, you'll have to take it out of my hide!"

Ben took a step forward to intervene, but before he could, the doctor let fly with the best punch he had delivered since he'd won the regimental bantam-weight boxing championship some twenty years earlier.

Dodger dropped like a pole-axed hog, and a cheer went up from the other customers.

The doctor bent down and felt for a heartbeat, checked his pulse, and tested Dodger's jaw for fracture. Satisfied, he stood up and pulled the invoice from his casebook. "Tiny: your back."

Tiny turned and bent forward to make a writing desk. The doctor laid the invoice on his back, produced the stub of a pencil, licked it and scrawled "Paid in Full" on the paper. Then he dropped it on Dodger's chest and made his way back to the buggy.

Ben watched him drive away. In his eyes, the little doctor seemed to have grown a lot taller.

37: A hard man

1900

Danny and Tommy, now around ten years old, were up in the big maple tree beside the barn when the wagon came rattling down the road. A big team of Clydesdales was pulling it, but that wasn't what caught their attention. Four shaggy ponies were tied side by side to the tailgate—two blacks and two dark bays, not as small as Shetlands or Welsh but a long way from being as big as horses.

The wagon appeared to be turning into the smithy so the boys scrambled down out of the tree and headed over for a closer look. When they got around to the front of the shop they found Ben in conversation with the driver of the wagon.

"These here are the last of the little brutes we hauled over from Sable Island," the man seated on the wagon was saying. "We sold sixteen of them right off the barge at Hall's Harbour, but these buggers were kicking up such a fuss, everybody was afraid of them. I'm dragging them over to the train station and shipping them off to Cape Breton. They'll be able to use them in the coal mines."

Spying Danny and Tommy approaching, the man shouted, "You boys stay away from their hind ends, especially those bays. They're so mean they can kick you and bite you at the same time!"

Ben went over to the boys and, wrapping his arms around them, ushered them toward the house. "Go on in and get yourselves a couple of the cookies your mothers baked this morning."

"But we want to see!" Danny said.

"You can watch from the porch. I need to talk to this fellow without you adding your opinions."

Lilly had seen the wagon arriving and as she handed the boys their treats, she said to no one in particular, "I hope that man doesn't want Ben to try to shoe those ponies. They're still wild. He'll get himself hurt."

She needn't have worried. Ben had no intention of touching the ponies, at least not yet. He had other plans.

He knew Danny and Tommy were both longing for horses of their own. They'd been riding the legs off his poor old gelding. Old Charley had assumed that he was retired, until the boys started riding him, doubled up and bareback, for hours at a time. Finally, in protest, Charley had refused to leave the yard while they were on his back.

Not deterred, the boys would simply get off and lead him a mile or so down the road, then mount up there. They knew the old fellow wouldn't be able to resist the attraction of his quiet stall back home. At regular intervals they would come whooping into the yard as fast as they could make Charley canter.

Eventually Ben was forced to limit this activity,

The Secret of the Spring

scolding the boys and apologizing to the old horse as he frequently had to rescue him and lead him away to safety.

Now he was looking speculatively at the ponies. The blacks seemed to be in good shape, but the bays were gaunt-looking. Their manes and tails were long and full of burrs. The hair on their flanks and rumps was matted with manure and their legs were swollen and bruised. There were bright red oozing abrasions where they must have fallen in the barge when she hit the rough weather in the bay. The man on the wagon should've been ashamed of himself for dragging them along in that state.

Ben kept his opinion to himself. He didn't want to get the man's back up now that he was planning to make him an offer. Maybe he was crazy, maybe he should be as reticent as the buyers over at the shore had been and simply let the ponies move on. He tried to talk himself out of it but found the words coming out of his mouth anyway.

"Those bays are looking pretty poorly. They probably won't make it all the way over to Sydney. I might be a fool, but if the price is right, I might take them off your hands."

Ben could just as easily have made an offer on the blacks—they were in better shape—but there was something about the other pair, something in their eyes that made his heart go out to them.

"I'll give you the pair for thirty dollars," the man on the wagon opened up with.

Ben just chuckled and made to walk away. "I thought you were serious about selling them."

He had only made a few paces toward the smithy when the man piped up again. "Hang on a minute, Ben. I'm a reasonable man. Make me an offer."

"I'll make you an offer, but it will be firm and final, so don't waste my time trying to dicker with me," Ben exclaimed, pretending to be angry. Then with a look that said the negotiations were over, he brazenly said, "Eight dollars apiece, take it or leave it."

The man on the wagon looked truly hurt, but after looking over his shoulder at the ponies several more times and scratching his whiskers, he turned back to Ben. "You're a hard man, Ben Johnson. I guess I'll take your offer and I'd like to say I wish you luck with them, but I guess I won't. If you or them boys get hurt, don't come crying to me."

He climbed down off the wagon and, with help from Ben and a half a dozen customers from the smithy who had been standing around witnessing the transaction, managed to get the ponies, kicking, rearing and plunging, into separate box stalls in the barn. Ben paid the man his sixteen dollars and watched him take his leave, heading to Middleton and hoping to encounter another sucker along the way.

Ben stood in the stable, watching the ponies circling around exploring their enclosures, testing the walls and looking for an escape route. He knew it would be a while before they settled down. He hoped his instincts were correct and that the ponies would respond the way he hoped they would. Handled properly and given the chance, wild unspoiled horses made wonderfully dependable mounts. It was all in the way you brought them along. He was no novice in that regard—breaking in remounts had been part of his responsibilities with the 17th.

There had been nothing wilder and more unmanageable than those Basuto ponies in South Africa that they'd herded right off the Veld to replace the regiment's horses that had been lost at sea. Still, under the careful hands of men who knew their business, the little horses were trooping along with the regular mounts in less than a month. He had had the same experience in India when they were short of horses and had to use the wild Manipuri and Chamurti horses.

He was still standing wondering if he had done the right thing when the boys burst through the stable door. Ben put up his big hand and stopped them in their tracks.

He pushed them back out the door and when he had them in the yard and quiet, he laid out the rules: "These animals are wild and scared, and it's going to take a lot of time and work to get them quieted down and trusting us. Until I get them to the point that I feel they're safe, I don't want either one of you anywhere near them. If you think you can do as I say and stay away from them, then we'll keep them. You'll have to promise me. And if you break that promise, I'll take the ponies down to Middleton and put them on the train. They'll have to work as pit ponies in Cape Breton. What's it going to be?"

"I swear," Danny said.

"Promise," Tommy echoed.

As it turned out, despite many temptations, they kept their word. Ben got the vet to help him castrate the little stallions and attend to their injuries. Then he spent a full month working with the animals: running his hands over them; teaching them to lead properly; picking up their feet so he could trim them; getting them used to carrying light weights on their backs; and, finally, using a harness he'd made, hitching them to a drag and then a small wagon. Then and only then did he let the boys get involved.

He introduced them to the ponies slowly, letting them groom them, lead them around, pick up their feet and generally establish a rapport.

"You can draw straws," he said, "to see who gets which pony."

The boys exchanged a glance. Then Danny said, "We agreed. They came together, so we'll share them. Both of them belong to both of us."

Ben gave them a long look. "That's about the smartest thing I've heard this year," he said at last.

Under Ben's care the little horses recuperated from their injuries. They gained weight and their wounds healed and haired over.

Within a few days after he allowed the boys to attack their ponies with curry combs and brushes, their coats had taken on show horse sheen. Earlier,

The Secret of the Spring

they had all been surprised to discover that, after Ben removed some of the mud, manure and blood, each pony had a white star on its forehead and one white stocking. Now the markings stood out in bright contrast to the glistening bay bodies and shiny black manes and tails.

Finally the day came when Ben felt it was time to try the boys and the ponies together. Ben and Alphonse each held a pony while Danny and Tommy climbed off the mounting block onto their bare backs. The boys were excited and squirming around more than Ben would have liked but to his relief, the ponies didn't seem to mind.

"Sit very still," he said in a calm voice. "If they get excited and throw you, it won't just hurt you when you hit the ground. It will mean a lot longer training until they get over the fright."

Once Ben was convinced that both boys and ponies were going to behave themselves, the two fathers took them for a long walk up the road, holding the halters close as the ponies got used to this new adventure.

After a couple of miles everybody started to relax. The men stayed close to the ponies' heads but let go of the halters and surrendered the reins to the boys.

They walked on into the morning, the men discussing a hunting trip they were planning and the boys leaning forward like jockeys and speculating on the speed of their mounts.

"I have never spent much time with horses," Alphonse said. "How old do you think these two are?"

"I checked their teeth when they first came, after I got them quieted down a bit. I'm happy to say the one by you is five years old, and this one is around six."

"This is a good thing?"

"It means they have their whole lives ahead of them. Sable Island ponies live a long time. There's one a fellow has not far from here. It doesn't work any more, but it's enjoying a good life at thirty-five years old."

He slapped Alphonse on the back, saying, "Hell, if they don't get sick or injured they'll outlive both of us!"

When they reached the intersection where the hotel had once stood, Ben suggested to the boys that they dismount and take their ponies over to the spring for a drink. With a laugh he added, "Maybe they'll come back as full sized horses!"

Alphonse didn't laugh – he didn't like it when anybody joked about the powers of the spring.

"They weren't thirsty," the boys offered as they led their mounts back up to the road.

"I guess that's why they're still the same size," Ben suggested in a second attempt at his joke.

"You can lead a horse to water but you can't make him drink," Alphonse offered wryly, knowing Ben would catch his double meaning.

The boys, in true form, swapped ponies for the trip home.

After a few more outings of this kind, the fathers stepped back and the boys were left to their own devices. During the rest of the summer, when they weren't doing their chores or setting rabbit snares up on the mountain, Danny and Tommy were constantly on their ponies' backs, exploring or pretending to be members of Ben's old regiment, charging imaginary foes with the crude lances they'd whittled.

Ben wasn't sure how he felt about the boys playing at war. He knew it was his fault. They had sat around the fire with him when Lilly pushed him to tell them about his past. He had told and retold the old stories of his time with his regiment. He had tried to show the futility of all that he had experienced, but somehow they had only absorbed the glorious aspects of the yarns.

The boys had also begun helping him by using their ponies to yard short firewood logs out of the woodlot and to drag small cocks of hay over to the barn. Late one summer day as Ben leaned on his hayfork, watching them pretending to be men, geeing and hawing their ponies around, he said a silent prayer. "Please, God, let me live to see the boys lead the kind of lives where these skills are more important to them than the other ones they've been practising."

38: Made his toes curl

1902

Ben, with Danny and Tommy on either side, came bursting through the kitchen door. The boys were sniggering and guffawing.

"Now what's got into you two clowns?" Lilly said. She was pleased to see them so happy. She and Angie had prepared lunch and set the table and they were busy passing dishes and bowls from the warming oven.

Alphonse was away peddling and Danny and Tommy had been out working with Ben for the morning. Neither boy showed much aptitude or interest in blacksmithing or the farrier trade, but they were always eager to help out. They occasionally served as Ben's strikers. It was a simple job—all they needed to do was heft the sledge hammer and rhythmically pound whatever piece of red-hot metal Ben placed on the anvil.

Danny giggled. "You won't believe the story old Pete Mosher was trying to get us to believe this morning, Mom. You tell her, Dad."

"Well, it was pretty funny, Lil," Ben began. "You know how Pete is kind of loose with the truth, but this morning he came up with a real whopper."

"More stories about them women up on South Mountain?"

"Not this time. He had a story from back when the Spa Springs Hotel was in full swing."

Lilly turned away, pretending to attend to something on the stove. Angie stopped fussing with the jar of preserves she was trying to open and shot a concerned look toward Lilly while Ben, oblivious, continued his story.

"Pete was bragging that he had the best damned trout stream in the Valley, but that in some ways it was a curse. The brook runs through his pasture and fishermen were always going in and disturbing his cows, then leaving and not closing the gate properly."

Ben knew that that part of the story was true. He and Alphonse, and sometimes Doctor Rutledge, would fish there themselves...but always with Pete's permission.

"But then he says that, one day, all of his cows showed up back at the barn right after he'd taken them out to the pasture. He had a good idea what had happened—some damned fishermen had left the gate open again. He said he was mad as hell and fumed all the way down to the pasture and, sure enough, the gate was open and the rig from the hotel was parked right there, with the team tied near the stream. There was a clutch of dandies with their lines dipped in the water."

"It was a hotel for the fancy folk," Lilly said quietly.

"Well, Pete said he went right over to them and gave the man who looked to be in charge a piece of his mind. You know what it means when Pete lets fly with a piece of his mind. But then he said that, after he finished tearing the man a new arse hole, one of the other men ran over to him and said, 'How dare you? You're talking to the Prince of Wales!' And what did Pete say to that, Danny?"

"He said, 'Is he, now? Well, I'm The Duke of York! Now get your asses off my property.' Tell Mom the rest, Dad."

Lilly kept her face turned away, seemingly very busy with something on the stove.

"Pete said that, just the other day he saw something that made his toes curl. He stopped at the town hall in Middleton to pay his taxes, and there's a new portrait of the King on the wall. And then what did he say, Tommy?"

"He said, 'By God, that's him, I never forget a face. It *was* the Prince Of Wales.'"

Ben and the boys began laughing again, repeating 'it *was* the Prince of Wales' to each other.

Finally Ben turned toward Lily. "Now isn't that the worst bit of nonsense you ever heard?"

Lilly dropped the spoon she had been stirring with and walked directly toward the stairwell.

"What's wrong? Are you all right, Lil?"

"I'm fine—just a little headache. I'm going upstairs to lie down for a while."

Angie passed Ben and the boys their plates, then filled Lilly's favourite tea cup and headed for the stairs.

"Maybe I should take that up to her?" Ben said.

"You men just finish your meal and get back to work. She'll be all right. It's just that time...you know."

Ben turned to his food, not really satisfied with Angie's explanation. Over the past couple of years Lilly had started acting a little strangely—not her usual bubbly self. For no apparent reason she would suddenly stop whatever she was doing and head off on her own for what she called her quiet time. Ben was worried about her and at a loss to explain her behaviour.

Angie was not. She knew exactly what had started it all.

Two years earlier Ben had rushed into the kitchen with a newspaper in his hands. He had just been to town. "The flags are all hanging at half-mast and everybody is upset. The queen has died, so I guess it's 'God save the King'."

Lilly listened to what Ben was saying, then, without saying a word, turned and headed upstairs for the first of what had become her quiet times.

Since that time the episodes had become frequent. Each time they occurred Angie would instruct a baffled Ben to sit tight while she went to comfort Lilly.

Angie would go up and sit talking quietly to her as Lilly lay unresponsive staring at the ceiling. It took Angie back to the time when she had sat at Lilly's side when they worked together at the hotel.

Lilly had the safety of Ben's strong arms at night and Angie's shoulder to lean on during the day, and

205

her bad memories would begin to fade until something more would happen to reignite them.

In 1902, when all the talk was about the Coronation and Danny and Tommy brought their small Edward VII prints home from school to show her, she was just able to manage a smile before retreating upstairs.

The following year she was in the store in Kingston, settling up for her purchases and enjoying some friendly conversation with the clerk. Then he passed her a newly-minted coin as change. As small as it was, his profile on the penny left her dumbfounded and acting so strangely that the clerk summoned Ben over to assist her back to their buggy.

As it turned out, those coins were therapeutic. She and Angie kept tabs on all of Ben's earnings, and each evening they would count the day's money, put it into a strongbox, and record the amounts in the journal. At first Lilly handled the new coins as if they had been heated in the forge, barely daring to touch them. But gradually, at Angie's insistence, she kept at it until, over time and with repetition, the image became so commonplace it no longer pressed into her heart. It became just another face on a coin.

With Angie's help she had found a way to deal with her demon, but occasionally, as when Ben told Pete's story, she would find herself slipping back into that place of safety she had discovered so long ago.

39: The world is not as it was

One day a man from away visited Ben with an interesting proposal. He introduced himself as Andrew Stewart, the project manager for the MacDonald Tobacco Company and in charge of the construction and staffing of the new consolidated school in Middleton.

"Oh, yes?" Ben said as he put down his tools and wiped his hands.

He knew everybody in the surrounding area was excited about the new facility. The complex of buildings, dominated by a massive, three story red brick school, was going to bring their children's education up to the standards of the new century. All the one-room schools situated reasonably close to the new institution were to close, and the children of the area were to be transported to and from their homes daily.

Ben wasn't sure how he felt about the scheme. Danny and Tommy had mostly been schooled at home, only attending the small school down the road when it was convenient. Hector Sermon, the aging schoolmaster, was comfortable with the arrangement because he knew that both boys were better at reading, writing and doing their sums than any of their classmates. Ben was a literate man and Lilly, suffused with what he had taught her, had eagerly helped him pass the knowledge on to the boys.

Mr. Sermon, unlike other teachers in the Valley, had not been offered a position at the new school. The teacher from North Mountain School, Mr. Jones, whom Mr. Sermon felt had inferior qualifications, was to be vice principal.

Mr. Sermon had confessed to Ben, "It is hard to work so faithfully and so long, and then to suffer the insult of being overlooked like this."

"Is there aught you can do?"

"Were I younger, I would fight it," Mr. Sermon had said. "But I am seventy-five, you know. I must embrace the golden pleasures of retirement."

Ben looked upon this visit from Mr. Stewart as an opportunity to find out all he could about the new facility, but first he had to find out the reason for his visit.

"We will soon take receipt of several vans that we will use to transport the children to and from the school," Mr. Stewart said. "We have secured ten teams of suitable horses for the vans."

"They will need a ton of hay."

"They will. But at the moment they are in pasture, waiting to be shod. Then we can make them ready for the fall term."

Ben could see where the conversation was going. "There's a perfectly good blacksmith in town. No need to come out this far and, besides, I'm very busy these days. I don't just shoe horses and oxen, you know."

"Yes, I do know and that's one of the reasons that I've come to see you," Mr. Stewart said. "We also need sleigh runners made to replace the wheels on the vans for the winter, and Edmonds says he's not up to the task. He recommended you."

After a lot of jawing back and forth, Ben finally agreed to design and build the sleigh runners and share the maintenance of the horses with John Edmonds, the smith in town. He had also extracted enough information about the school to convince him that it might be a useful place for Danny to meet other children his own age and broaden his horizons.

He wanted to include Tommy, but he knew Alphonse would be reluctant to agree. For some reason Alphonse always gave a wide berth to Middleton and its citizens.

That night, as they sat around the fire at the camp on the mountain, Ben broached the subject with his friend, expecting a hard response.

But he saw Alphonse glance at Angie, who had her mouth shut tight but her eyes sending messages.

Alphonse looked at the fire, then down at his hands, and finally up at Ben. "I have been pondering it," he said. "The world is not as it was when I was small. Perhaps this new school could offer Tommy something of use."

Ben reached over and shook Alphonse's hand. "Our lads can bring home wonders to teach us old ones, perhaps."

On the first day of school, Ben and Lilly stood with

a reluctant pair of twelve-year-olds between them as the van from the MacDonald's Consolidated School pulled up in front of the blacksmith shop. Angie and Alphonse were standing on the veranda, watching with restrained excitement.

"All aboard!" the driver shouted for the tenth time that morning. He gave a friendly greeting and smiled as Ben urged Danny up onto the steps of the van.

Ben turned to Tommy. "Your turn now."

He gave the lad a hand up, not seeing how the driver's expression quickly changed.

The driver said no more. He watched over his shoulder as the boys took their seats, then moved the team on with a flick of reins.

Lilly and Angie were in the kitchen preparing the midday meal and discussing the new slates and lunch pails they were going to buy for the boys when they heard footsteps on the porch and the screen door swung open. The two boys entered and just stood together, staring at the floor.

"What the devil?" Angie said, glancing at the clock. "What are you boys doing home at this hour?"

Danny looked up with tears in his eyes. "Mr. Jones, he sent us home. He said there was schools for Tommy down river and that he wasn't about to waste his time with anyone related to the Leonard clan either. He said we could hang around town and get a ride back with the van later, but we didn't want to wait, so we walked."

Angie took the boys over to the table to calm and comfort them.

The Secret of the Spring

"What did Mr. Jones mean about—?"

"Don't worry about that for now, Danny," Lilly said, as she went out to find Ben.

Within ten minutes Ben had caught and saddled his horse and was cantering in the direction of Middleton. He knew he wasn't thinking clearly. He hadn't had a visit from his old demon for years but now he rode with him again, suggesting dire consequences for the insensitive teacher. This was the same man who had refused to accept Lilly years ago and now he had hurt the feelings of his precious boys. He didn't know what he was going to do to Mr. Jones, but it wasn't going to be pretty.

Fifteen minutes at a full-out canter brought him to the front steps of the school. If the doors at the top of the long staircase had been open, such was his rage that he might have ridden his horse all the way up and into the front hall.

He leapt from his saddle, tied his horse to the railing, took the steps two at a time, and at the door stopped abruptly to avoid colliding with Mr. Stewart.

"Whoa! Ben, what's your hurry?"

"Step aside, Mr. Stewart! I've no quarrel with you. Just tell me where I can find that bastard, Jones."

"I assume Mr. Jones is in a classroom with a full complement of impressionable children. Surely what you have to say to him can wait until after school?"

"I hadn't planned on talking to the man."

"What did you plan on doing?"

"I thought I'd start by erasing the blackboard with his face."

Stewart stepped back, shocked, then put out a calming hand. "Ben, would you do me the favour of taking a walk with me so you can tell me what's troubling you?"

Ben thought of pushing past the man, but he noticed a cluster of curious first graders walking toward them. He took in their innocent young faces and it was as if he had been doused with a bucket of the cold water of common sense.

The two men spent the better part of an hour walking side by side through the school grounds as Ben explained what had happened to his boys. When Ben had spoken his piece, the pair walked silently to where his horse stood waiting.

"Will you trust me to deal with this?" Stewart said.

Ben nodded reluctant assent, swung into the saddle and headed for home.

Alphonse and Angie joined Ben, Lilly and the boys for supper that evening but it was a quiet meal. Nobody wanted to talk about what had happened. The boys seemed to be looking to their parents for answers, but none were forthcoming.

The following afternoon Ben had a visit from a smiling and ingratiating Mr. Stewart. He climbed out of his buggy and immediately came over to offer his hand.

"I want to thank you for bearing with me yesterday, Ben. I know it must have seemed like I was trying to brush you off. That wasn't the case; there were things afoot that I couldn't tell you about then."

"Can you tell me now?"

The Secret of the Spring

"You may not know that our new school is the first of several that Sir William McDonald plans to fund and build across Canada. Sir William was actually on the premises himself when you showed up yesterday. He's a generous, modest man. He took in much of our initial encounter on the front steps and was only too eager to find out what we discussed on our stroll around the yard. In all the time I have worked for him, I have never seen Sir William angry. But after I disclosed what you told me, he flew into a rage."

Ben was aware of small faces staring at them from the kitchen window, so he drew Mr. Stewart toward the forge as the man continued.

"He started shouting that what Jones had said and done flew in the face of everything he was trying to accomplish. He said it was unacceptable and that he wasn't going to stand for it. When I offered to handle the matter myself, he refused and instead directed me to arrange a meeting; he wanted to confront Jones himself.

"I knew heads would roll, Ben, and by God, they did. I thought it was a little unusual for a Knight of the Realm to choose the area out behind the school barn as a suitable place for a meeting but it was his choice so I thought it was prudent to follow Jones as he made his way there after the children had all gone home.

"Sir William had had quite a bit of time to think matters over and I thought maybe Jones might get off with a stern reprimand, but when the bigoted bastard stopped to light his pipe before turning the corner at the rear of the barn, I knew his fate was sealed.

"You see, Ben, although Sir William is probably the richest man in Canada, and all that money has come from the sale of tobacco, strangely, the man detests the stuff himself. He thinks smoking or chewing it is a filthy habit and that anybody who uses it is a fool."

"But he sells the stuff, advertises it!"

"I know. Don't ask me to explain it. I stood out of sight but I could hear harsh words flying, and they were all coming out of Sir William's mouth. The outcome is that Mr. Jones is no longer with the school. Sir William has asked me to extend his humble apology and that the boys are welcome to return."

"Well!" Ben said. "That is more than I had expected."

"But no more than what is right." Stewart added, "And you should know I have just come from seeing Mr. Sermon. He has agreed to postpone his retirement for a while and to fill the empty position."

"This is more than satisfactory, Mr. Stewart."

Stewart smiled. "I wish all problems could be resolved so neatly."

As he was about to leave, Stewart noticed Ben looking at several cases of jugs stowed behind the seat in his buggy.

"Water from the spring," he said simply. "Sir William had me down there filling jugs for half the morning. He's taking it home with him and has instructed the school janitor to send him regular shipments of the stuff. I didn't know it, but he attended the spa several times before it burned down. I can't imagine what the old fellow thinks the tonic is going to do for him."

Garry Leeson

40: Gag a maggot

Ben was sitting with Lilly and Danny, telling stories of his exploits in some far-flung place at the other side of the world, when it occurred to him: his wife and son had never been further afield than the village of Kingston. That was only a few miles away, and they only went even that far when it was necessary.

It was his fault that their trips to towns were so infrequent, Ben thought. He never felt comfortable taking them to a place as populous as Middleton. He was proud of his beautiful wife and his healthy, robust son, but he was always worried that people would see him as an old rogue parading Lilly around like a trophy.

In recent years another problem had presented itself. Lilly's brother, Harold, now in his late thirties, had moved down off the mountain and established himself as Middleton's resident ne'er-do-well.

As a young man, Harold had simply been not too bright; but as he grew older, a rapidly progressing dementia took hold of him and he was becoming a real nuisance, imposing himself wherever people of the town gathered. He was hugely obese, his prematurely grey hair was long and dirty, and his matted beard always bore remnants of his most recent meal.

The Secret of the Spring

Unless he got caught out in the rain, his body never encountered water, and the stench that wafted around him was overpowering. As old Abe Mosher put it, "It was enough to gag a maggot!"

Harold had found an abandoned hobo shack down by the railway tracks and took up residence there. Using a borrowed wheelbarrow, he hauled enough horse manure from the livery stable to make a neat pile at the back of his shelter. This, with the addition of a few dirty wool blankets, became his bed in the winter. The heat from the rotting horse dung added to his comfort and the smell that clung to the several layers of clothing he always wore masked and, somehow, improved the odours that normally swirled around him during the summer months.

Harold's favourite haunt was the general store where, when he had the money, he would buy large quantities of raw wieners and eat them, on-site, two at a time. For hygienic reasons he had been banned from helping himself to the pickle jars and the cracker barrels, and the women at the shop would give him a handful at a time just to keep him at bay.

Harold fancied himself a poet, and would recite his nonsense rhymes to anyone brave enough to get within hearing distance. He was in the habit of talking with his mouth full, and accompanied his orations with a barrage of cracker crumbs and wiener bits.

"They're good verses," he would cry to the retreating backs of those he had just anointed. "Why won't you stay for more?"

Why he hadn't been scooped up and taken to the Poor Farm was a mystery to everyone who knew him. Ben had often thought of taking the initiative and reporting him to the authorities, but he wasn't sure how that would sit with Lilly, so he let sleeping dogs lie. Two years earlier, after Lilly's unexpected encounter with her brother on a shopping trip to town with Ben, she had flatly refused to ever set foot in the place again.

Because he had many business contacts in Middleton, Ben was forced to go there by himself; but for their monthly shopping trips for staples, the couple now opted to travel the few extra miles east to Kingston.

That's two places Lilly and the boy have been, no more, Ben mused. Then he started considering the matter more seriously.

When next he and Lilly were together, he blurted out, "I think it's time we took a trip, Lil. A real trip, not just a jaunt up the road to Kingston—a real, honest to goodness trip to some place you haven't been before. What would you say if I got us three tickets and we all took the Flying Bluenose to Halifax for a few days?"

"Oh, I don't know, Ben. You're so busy and I've just started canning and I don't really have anything to wear."

"Hang the shop, hang the canning and hang the dress. What the hell does it matter what the most beautiful girl in the Valley wears, anyway?"

He started to say he liked her better with nothing

The Secret of the Spring

on at all, but remembered that Danny was at the table and caught himself in time.

Lilly pursed her lips and he knew she knew exactly what he was thinking. There was a long, tense pause, and then she said slowly, "I suppose...if you give me a day or two...and if I could find some material, I could get Mrs. Neilly to help me whip up something suitable."

"Yes, by God, we'll go, then!" Ben thumped the table with his big fist and rubbed Danny's hair 'til the boy ducked away laughing.

A week later, the Neillys dropped them off at the Middleton station an hour before the train for Halifax was due. Their neighbours, in addition to taking them to the station, had also agreed to do their chores and milk their cow while they were away.

Ben hoped that they wouldn't encounter Harold during their short wait for the train but, true to form, he showed up. Fortunately he kept his distance while he bothered the other waiting passengers with his insane banter.

After an uncomfortably long wait they heard the whistle blowing in the distance and the train rolled into the station, spewing steam and smoke as it came to a slow screeching halt.

Before it was completely stopped, the conductor, dressed in a smart grey uniform, swung down from a door in the row of passenger cars and put a small step in place. "All aboard!" he shouted.

The passengers shuffled, luggage in hand, toward him. Ben, Lilly and Danny were the last to board. Ben was a seasoned traveller and he could see by the number of unoccupied windows that the cars were not very full. Lilly was looking a bit nervous and he didn't want to hurry her.

Once inside, Ben directed his little family to a pair of unoccupied bench seats where they could sit facing each other. As he slung the newly purchased leather suitcase up onto the overhead rack, they heard a series of metallic clicks and then the car lurched ahead.

Danny and Lilly took the seats closest to the window and peered through the smoky glass with ear-to-ear smiles on their faces. Seconds later, Lilly turned away frowning.

When Ben looked out the window to see what was bothering her, he saw her brother Harold shouting and waving to no one in particular.

While he watched, he heard a salesman in the seat behind them say, "I travel this route a lot and that crazy bugger is here every time the train goes by."

Ben and Lilly exchanged a look, but said nothing. They weren't going to let Harold spoil their trip.

Soon the passing scenery helped them recover their good humour. They pointed out odd-looking houses on the busy streets of the towns they passed through, and speculated on what all those people could be doing with their day.

When they arrived in Halifax they checked into a hotel that Doctor Rutledge had recommended, put their luggage in their room and set about seeing the town. They strolled down to the waterfront. When they had had enough walking, they boarded the trolley and a pair of lean bay horses pulled them along Water Street. They still had a good view of the harbour and the steamers and schooners tied up at the busy docks.

Ben was showing his family the city but actually he was seeing most of it for the first time himself. He'd only seen glimpses of it before boarding the train when he first arrived.

When the noon cannon on the Citadel announced the time, they headed back to the hotel and ordered lunch.

"Now, then," he said. "It is a traveller's rule to get the most exotic thing you can find on the menu."

"No, it's not," Lilly said. "I don't even know what they are."

It took patient wrangling, but Ben finally got Lilly and Danny to order meals that he thought would do justice to the occasion. The only thing they could agree on was dessert: ice cream. Once Danny got a taste of it, there was no stopping him. He had it with every meal and left to his own devices, would have dined exclusively on it.

Wandering along the streets of the city with his beautiful wife on his arm and their son at his side, Ben felt as if he were the luckiest man in the world. He had a good home, a thriving business and an uncommonly close friendship with the Arseneaus. He had finally found the peace he had been searching for. The Annapolis Valley and Nova Scotia had lived up to the promises.

Garry Leeson

The horrors of his previous life were starting to fade away.

41: It is all I have

A full moon lit the road ahead of him as Alphonse made his way toward Spa Springs. He was worried.

It had happened twice now—Angie had come to him and he'd found himself unable to respond. He'd never had a problem like that before, even back in the worst of his drinking days. If a chance arose, so did he.

Angie had been very understanding and just joked about it, but, at his age, it was no joke to him. That's why he was heading up the road in the dead of night, with a jug in hand.

People with the same problem had come from all over the world to take the cure at the spring, and they always went away claiming that it worked. He had been skeptical in the past, but now he was desperate.

He was doing this at night because he didn't want anyone to see him at the spring. He felt like he was stealing the water, and that irked him because that spring rightfully belonged to everyone.

He left the road and made his way to where the water flowed out of a boxed-in well on the slope above the small brook, and bent over to fill his jug. The air was belching loudly out of the container as it filled, and he didn't hear anything else until a twig snapped directly behind him.

As he pulled the jug away he felt something hard poke him in his back.

"Caught ya!" someone shouted. "And I thought yous Frenchies was hard to sneak up on."

Alphonse panicked for a moment, and then recognized the voice of the person who was holding a rifle to his back.

Pete Zink was a younger man he had shared many a bottle with before he met Angie. He wasn't really a friend; in fact, he was probably the last fellow Alphonse wanted to meet.

Pete was huge and muscular. He already had a bad reputation as a drunkard and a bully who did what he wanted in town because no one there was brave enough to stand up to him. Back when Alphonse was still drinking and kept a good supply of shine hidden away somewhere, Pete was always 'a friend indeed', but since he had taken up with Angie and changed his ways, their paths hadn't crossed.

Pete swung his gun away from Alphonse's back and let him get to his feet. He placed his free arm over Alphonse's shoulder and said. "C'mon up the mountain apiece. Me an' some of the boys are up at Skeeter's shack."

Skeeter was a bit of a hermit. He had built a small lean-to and squat on the property once owned by the Spa Springs Hotel. Since Captain Jacobs had left in disgrace, nobody was sure who owned the property, so nobody was troubled by his presence.

"I'd like to, Pete, but no can do," Alphonse said. "I got to get back to Angie."

"So you're too good for your old buddies now that you've started hanging out with that stuck-up blacksmith."

"No, it's not that—"

Pete swung the rifle around and pointed it directly at him. "I said you was going to come'n say hello to your old friends and, by God, you better!"

Alphonse could smell the moonshine on the man's breath and decided he was serious. He put his jug of water down and walked in the direction that Pete indicated. He figured he would only stay with them a while and, when they were too drunk to notice, he would slip away, get his jug and return home. He knew old Skeeter didn't like company unless they happened to have a jug or two with them, so when the liquor was gone, he'd be calling the party to a close.

As they left the woods and started into a clearing, they came upon a wagon with its team tied to the trees. Alphonse knew that neither Pete nor any of his cronies owned a rig like it, and figured somebody in town was going to be pretty angry when they checked their wagon shed and stable in the morning.

In addition to Skeeter, who was occupying the only chair, there were three men of various ages and stages of inebriation sitting around a campfire in front of the shanty. Alphonse knew them all, and what he knew was not reassuring. He said hello to each of them as he moved into the light of the campfire and they recognized him.

After the forced amenities were over, Pete came right to the point. It was apparent that they had a problem. The night was young and they had run out of liquor. "It's real lucky I run into you tonight, Phonsie boy, cuz I know you always got some shine stashed away around here. Me 'n' the boys are sorely in need. You wouldn't let your old friends down now, would ya, old Phonsie-boy?'

"The thing is, Pete, I haven't been drinking for some time now. I don't have any booze—"

The rifle barrel smashed into the side of Alphonse's head and he fell to his knees.

"Now that's mighty greedy and unsociable of you, Phonsie-boy. I knows you're lyin', so why don't you just tell us where the stuff is? One of the boys can get it and we can all be friends again."

"I'm not lying, Pete. There isn't any. My woman doesn't put up with it."

One of the other men got to his feet, stepped forward and kicked Alphonse in the face. He shouted, "God-damned lying frog, you'll tell me where it is or I'll kill you."

"Now settle down, Runt!" Pete shouted. "He'll tell us. You other fellas drag him over and tie him to that tree."

Once the men had him secured, Pete stood close in front of him. "Listen, Phonsie-boy, I hear that woman of yours is quite a looker. How's about you tell me where your camp is and I'll send the boys over for her and we'll have ourselves a party?"

"Truly I don't have any booze, but I've got some money in my pouch. You can head to town and buy some from Smiley."

Pete ripped the rawhide pouch from around Alphonse's waist and weighed it in his hand. "It ain't much."

"It is all I have."

Pete slowly counted the coins by the light of the fire, then nodded. "I guess it'll keep us 'til you come to your senses and tell us where you're hiding the good stuff."

He turned to his friends. "You boys hitch the team to the wagon and throw him into the back. We're headin' to town. Skeeter, too."

"I've had enough for tonight!" the hermit cried. But the men tossed him, kicking and complaining, up into the wagon box beside Alphonse, whose arms were tied behind him.

They pushed the horses as hard as they could down the hill to Middleton and, when they arrived at the bootlegger's place, left them sweating and gasping for breath at the side of the road while they went in to bargain with Smiley.

Alphonse twisted and turned in the wagon box trying to free himself, but the knots would not give.

The money didn't last long; Smiley was out of shine, and the group had to drink, and pay for, the more expensive legal stuff.

After a while Pete and his buddies emerged from

the ramshackle house to resume the interrogation of Alphonse. He pleaded with them, telling them that there was no hidden liquor but they wouldn't listen.

Pete turned the horses back toward the North Mountain, while two of the boys took turns kicking Alphonse in the ribs and demanding answers. When old Skeeter tried to suggest that Alphonse had had enough, he got a quick backhand in the face for his trouble.

"I'll decide who does what around here, you old fool!" Pete said.

Further up the road, the horses shortened their stride as the wagon rattled over the railway tracks. Pete had been half asleep up on the seat, but the jarring stirred him and he had an inspiration.

He wheeled the horses onto the road that ran parallel to the tracks and followed it for about a mile. The boys were curious as to what he had in mind so they let off kicking Alphonse for a while.

Pete reined in the horses at a spot beyond town limits and climbed down from the wagon. "Now boys, I'm going to show you how to make a Frenchie talk. You see, we gotta let him know we're serious when we ask a simple question like, 'where ya got your liquor hidden?' We need a sure-fire way of getting him to cooperate. Runt: you and Sam haul him off the wagon and tie him over that railway track. There's a train due before daylight, but I'm sure he'll start remembering where the liquor is before then."

Alphonse fought with everything he could, lashing

out with his bound legs and butting with his head, but nothing he could do stopped them.

"As soon as you tell us what we wanna know, we'll cut you loose and you can go back to that woman of yours," Pete said, looking down from the wagon seat. "Aw, he's already crying, boys. It won't be long now."

Pete urged the horses a little further along to where there was a clearing in a stand of trees. He climbed down off the wagon, stretching and belching.

"I'm going to get a little shuteye. You stay awake and listen. When Alphonse decides to be reasonable, wake me up."

"Then what happens?"

"Then he tells us where the stuff is and we give him a ride back up the mountain. You know he's a little stubborn, but he's really not such a bad fella."

They all had a chuckle and Pete found a soft spot and drifted off to sleep.

He woke to the sound of a train whistle in the distance. As he looked around, he saw the other men were coming awake.

The bastards all went to sleep, he cursed to himself as he rolled over and got to his feet.

Seconds later they heard the scream and the shrieks of the train's brakes. Then they heard a wet thud as Alphonse's head and torso landed on their side of the tracks.

The mangled corpse quivered and contorted in the gravel and Alphonse's head lolled over wide-eyed, looking at them accusingly. The horses spooked and took off at a gallop, dragging the empty wagon behind them.

With Pete in the lead, the terrified men ran through the woods until they came to a small clearing, where they stopped to catch their breath.

"You boys get yourselves home as fast as you can," Pete ordered. "Nobody saw us tonight. You weren't here and this never happened. We're in the clear. If one of yous ever breathes a word of this to anyone, I'll personally tie *you* to the tracks."

The younger men headed back to their homes in town and old Skeeter hoofed it back up to his shack on the mountain.

When it was day, Pete headed out to find the three younger men to make sure they stayed true to the deal, but they had all left town. With his big hunting knife hidden under the loose jacket he wore, he headed up the hill to pay Skeeter a visit. He was prepared to do what he felt was necessary, but when he got there, he found the old man sitting in his shack naked, mumbling to himself.

Pete slapped him around a bit, but he soon realized the old codger was out of his mind and no threat—even if he did talk, no one would believe him.

Pete left the knife in its sheath and headed back to town. He carried on to Reverend Mackay and put a bee in his ear about Skeeter, just to make sure the old man wouldn't be a problem. A wagon wasn't long coming from the Poor Farm to transport the raving old man to the home further up the Valley.

The Secret of the Spring

Once the memory of that terrible night started to fade, Pete decided that it had not been a bad bit of work. He'd had some fun, rid himself of Skeeter, and gained possession of the little shack near the spring.

42: But lips were sealed

Ben and Lilly got the news soon after lunch.

Ben was already at work, shoeing a huge brindle ox. The beast was suspended in the stocks with all four feet off the ground, and he had only attended to two of the cloven hooves when Collins, the town constable, came flying into the yard in his buggy. He tied up his sweat-lathered horse and pushed his way past the men assembled at the smithy, going directly over to Ben.

"I need a word," he said quietly.

Ben gave him a long look, put down his tools, and led Collins to the back of the building. He leaned in close to the constable, heard what Collins had to say, and stayed in that position as if frozen for a long minute.

Collins started to speak again, but Ben shook his head. He undid his leather apron, dropped it over a barrel, walked unspeaking through the crowd, and turned toward his house.

"What about my ox?" its owner cried.

Ben seemed not to hear, leaving the man and his beast hanging.

He had tears in his eyes when he told Lilly what had happened. The constable had been brutally honest, but Ben spared his wife the gruesome details.

The Secret of the Spring

"I need to go up to the camp," he said. "Somebody has to break the news to Angie and her boy."

"No," Lilly said, wiping her eyes. "It should be me."

"I didn't want to ask you, but it would help if you did that. I have to go look to the body."

She hugged him fiercely. "I don't want anything to happen to you."

"It's just a trip to the funeral home."

He hitched his horse to his buckboard and headed to town, leaving several teamsters kicking stones in his yard and a half-shod ox bellowing in the stocks.

When Ben got to the funeral home, on a side road west of the town, there were several buggies tied up outside and men were lined up near the rear door. At first he thought there must be another funeral going on, but as he climbed down from his wagon, he realized that these people were not grieving. Sensing what was going on, he pushed his way through the door, past a woman sitting at a table with a money box in front of her, and down the flight of stairs to the basement.

It was a brightly-lit room with a high ceiling. The walls were fitted with shelves of bottles of multi-coloured liquids and polished brass containers. Strange paraphernalia stood among red rubber hoses and big needles on a table nearby.

Circles of men were crowded around a large, marble-topped table near the centre of the room. As Ben moved toward them he heard a voice.

"Gentlemen," the undertaker was saying, "what

you are looking at is, without a doubt, the strangest cadaver that has ever graced my facility."

There was a murmur of nervous laughter.

"And worth every penny of admission my good wife is charging at the door—which, I assure you, will go toward the cost of seeing the departed suitably interred."

He gestured toward the table. "Notice that our friend here has been sliced neatly into three pieces, but that I have successfully put them back together."

"No!" Ben bellowed in anger.

The crowd around the table parted, exposing the mutilated and naked body of his friend on the cold, white stone.

He stood transfixed for a moment, then swung around to face the crowd. "Get out, you bastards, get out!"

Within seconds the room was cleared, men bunching up in the doorway and clambering over each other to avoid his wrath. They all knew him and knew what he was capable of.

The undertaker, who had been among the first to head for the stairs, recovered his poise enough to return to plead his case. "Now see here, Ben. I was just trying to make the best of a bad situation. Funerals don't come cheap, you know. I heard this, uh, poor man had no family, so I figured the community would like to defray some of the cost. It was only polite to let them have a look at what they were paying for."

"You decided on a sideshow, you bastard." Ben

The Secret of the Spring

grabbed the back of the undertaker's jacket and ushered him up the stairs to where his wife cowered behind the little table, the moneybox clutched to her bosom. The door was open and Ben could see that the crowd had retreated to a safe distance, but were still determined to see a show.

Ben grabbed the moneybox and hurled the coins into the front yard. "Shove your dirty money up your arses!"

He didn't wait to see the crowd's reaction; he grabbed the undertaker again and forced him back down the stairs.

The crowd had a merry scrabble for the coins, with not a few bloody noses sustained. Then, as it seemed like the fun was over, the men took themselves off to other entertainments.

Later that day, people peeping through closed curtains saw Ben slowly guide his wagon out of town. A fine oak coffin rested in the back. The undertaker, weak with fear, had tried to waive payment, but Ben had dropped the money for his services on the floor of the brightly-lit room.

They buried Alphonse at his campsite, and a bereft Angie and her son moved down to the house. Ben made repeated visits to the constable and the town's mayor, trying to seek some justice for his friend.

But lips were sealed and no justice was to be had.

Garry Leeson

43: Journey into darkness

1914

There was an air of excitement in the group of men who gathered at the forge that morning. Britain had finally declared war on Germany and the rumour was that all the Commonwealth militias that had been on standby for months were going to be called up.

Most of the men were worked up and spewing bold oaths. Old Pete Mosher, who was now in his nineties, set the tone, telling the boys what he would do, "by God, to those lousy Krauts, if only they would give me an age exemption and send me over."

"At your age, we'd be lucky to get you as far as Middleton," one of the boys offered.

The men had a good hoot at Old Pete's expense, but Ben and two others remained silent. There was nothing funny about the prospect of war to them. Ben had witnessed horrors in places these men hadn't even heard of, and the two men exchanging sober glances with him were veterans of the recent Boer War. Ben knew that most of these men had, like him, taken the trouble to travel to Canning in 1903 when they unveiled Borden's statue.

Didn't they see the tears on the widows' faces? Didn't they see the war-wounded with missing limbs?

The Secret of the Spring

Once the memory of that terrible night started to fade, Pete decided that it had not been a bad bit of work. He'd had some fun, rid himself of Skeeter, and gained possession of the little shack near the spring.

42: But lips were sealed

Ben and Lilly got the news soon after lunch.

Ben was already at work, shoeing a huge brindle ox. The beast was suspended in the stocks with all four feet off the ground, and he had only attended to two of the cloven hooves when Collins, the town constable, came flying into the yard in his buggy. He tied up his sweat-lathered horse and pushed his way past the men assembled at the smithy, going directly over to Ben.

"I need a word," he said quietly.

Ben gave him a long look, put down his tools, and led Collins to the back of the building. He leaned in close to the constable, heard what Collins had to say, and stayed in that position as if frozen for a long minute.

Collins started to speak again, but Ben shook his head. He undid his leather apron, dropped it over a barrel, walked unspeaking through the crowd, and turned toward his house.

"What about my ox?" its owner cried.

Ben seemed not to hear, leaving the man and his beast hanging.

He had tears in his eyes when he told Lilly what had happened. The constable had been brutally honest, but Ben spared his wife the gruesome details.

The Secret of the Spring

"I need to go up to the camp," he said. "Somebody has to break the news to Angie and her boy."

"No," Lilly said, wiping her eyes. "It should be me."

"I didn't want to ask you, but it would help if you did that. I have to go look to the body."

She hugged him fiercely. "I don't want anything to happen to you."

"It's just a trip to the funeral home."

He hitched his horse to his buckboard and headed to town, leaving several teamsters kicking stones in his yard and a half-shod ox bellowing in the stocks.

When Ben got to the funeral home, on a side road west of the town, there were several buggies tied up outside and men were lined up near the rear door. At first he thought there must be another funeral going on, but as he climbed down from his wagon, he realized that these people were not grieving. Sensing what was going on, he pushed his way through the door, past a woman sitting at a table with a money box in front of her, and down the flight of stairs to the basement.

It was a brightly-lit room with a high ceiling. The walls were fitted with shelves of bottles of multi-coloured liquids and polished brass containers. Strange paraphernalia stood among red rubber hoses and big needles on a table nearby.

Circles of men were crowded around a large, marble-topped table near the centre of the room. As Ben moved toward them he heard a voice.

"Gentlemen," the undertaker was saying, "what

you are looking at is, without a doubt, the strangest cadaver that has ever graced my facility."

There was a murmur of nervous laughter.

"And worth every penny of admission my good wife is charging at the door—which, I assure you, will go toward the cost of seeing the departed suitably interred."

He gestured toward the table. "Notice that our friend here has been sliced neatly into three pieces, but that I have successfully put them back together."

"No!" Ben bellowed in anger.

The crowd around the table parted, exposing the mutilated and naked body of his friend on the cold, white stone.

He stood transfixed for a moment, then swung around to face the crowd. "Get out, you bastards, get out!"

Within seconds the room was cleared, men bunching up in the doorway and clambering over each other to avoid his wrath. They all knew him and knew what he was capable of.

The undertaker, who had been among the first to head for the stairs, recovered his poise enough to return to plead his case. "Now see here, Ben. I was just trying to make the best of a bad situation. Funerals don't come cheap, you know. I heard this, uh, poor man had no family, so I figured the community would like to defray some of the cost. It was only polite to let them have a look at what they were paying for."

"You decided on a sideshow, you bastard." Ben

Garry Leeson

43: Journey into darkness
1914

There was an air of excitement in the group of men who gathered at the forge that morning. Britain had finally declared war on Germany and the rumour was that all the Commonwealth militias that had been on standby for months were going to be called up.

Most of the men were worked up and spewing bold oaths. Old Pete Mosher, who was now in his nineties, set the tone, telling the boys what he would do, "by God, to those lousy Krauts, if only they would give me an age exemption and send me over."

"At your age, we'd be lucky to get you as far as Middleton," one of the boys offered.

The men had a good hoot at Old Pete's expense, but Ben and two others remained silent. There was nothing funny about the prospect of war to them. Ben had witnessed horrors in places these men hadn't even heard of, and the two men exchanging sober glances with him were veterans of the recent Boer War. Ben knew that most of these men had, like him, taken the trouble to travel to Canning in 1903 when they unveiled Borden's statue.

Didn't they see the tears on the widows' faces? Didn't they see the war-wounded with missing limbs?

grabbed the back of the undertaker's jacket and ushered him up the stairs to where his wife cowered behind the little table, the moneybox clutched to her bosom. The door was open and Ben could see that the crowd had retreated to a safe distance, but were still determined to see a show.

Ben grabbed the moneybox and hurled the coins into the front yard. "Shove your dirty money up your arses!"

He didn't wait to see the crowd's reaction; he grabbed the undertaker again and forced him back down the stairs.

The crowd had a merry scrabble for the coins, with not a few bloody noses sustained. Then, as it seemed like the fun was over, the men took themselves off to other entertainments.

Later that day, people peeping through closed curtains saw Ben slowly guide his wagon out of town. A fine oak coffin rested in the back. The undertaker, weak with fear, had tried to waive payment, but Ben had dropped the money for his services on the floor of the brightly-lit room.

They buried Alphonse at his campsite, and a bereft Angie and her son moved down to the house. Ben made repeated visits to the constable and the town's mayor, trying to seek some justice for his friend.

But lips were sealed and no justice was to be had.

The Secret of the Spring

It was just a game to them, something to think about and bring them a little excitement as they went about the drudgery on their farms and in the woods.

Most of them, like Ben himself, were too old to go —but they had sons, and that was what was bothering him the most. As the mindless chatter of the men continued, Ben envisioned Danny and Tommy in uniform.

Finally, he lost his temper and decided he couldn't listen to any more of it. He slammed his hammer down with such force that it sent up a shower of sparks that caused the men around him to draw back. The red-hot shoe he had been forming split in half and was rendered useless.

All were silent as Ben regained his composure, retrieved the broken pieces with his tongs, cooled them in the water bucket and tossed them on the scrap heap. After that, the conversation took a different tone. He had made his point.

Danny and Tommy were now both in their twenties, grown men who had been on their own for over five years now. They were both still single, and if the news had made its way up to the logging camp where they were working, they would probably be chomping at the bit to join up. In fact, they didn't need to join up—they'd been in the militia and training as soldiers for a portion of every year since they were eighteen.

They came home to help with the haying, and filled the woodshed for winter. They were sure to be home at Christmas and other occasions, but other than that, they spent their time hunting and trapping, working as lumberjacks or on military training. In the years since he had been given the task, Sir Robert Borden had rebuilt the Canadian Reserves and promoted a culture that saw most of the young men in the Valley participating as part-time soldiers.

The timber trade was in full swing, and good work had moved closer to home for the boys. S.S. Stevens of Kingston had begun logging an area on the South Mountain around Randall Lake and was hiring every available man in the area to help him meet the demand for his high-quality, old-growth lumber. The wages he was offering reflected his higher profits.

Ever since they were both barely sixteen, Danny and Tommy had spent most of their winters far away in the logging camps along the Mersey River, whose waters spilled into the Atlantic at Liverpool on the province's South Shore. However, with the promise of almost double the wages, they were persuaded to wield their axes a little closer to home.

It wasn't just the extra money that attracted them, though. They'd heard about the incredible five-mile long flume that floated the sawn lumber out of the woods and down to the millpond at Rockville Notch. Everybody said it was an incredible feat of engineering and they were looking forward to seeing it in action.

During the coldest months of the year, all the choppers and teamsters stayed in the camp full time. The only news they got from the outside world was

The Secret of the Spring

from the close-by Cole Settlement or the hamlet of Harmony. When the roads and swamps were frozen enough to support their bob sleighs, the men from those places would haul loads of loose hay and feed for the hundred or so horses at the camp. They weren't required to bring much in the way of food for the men. Barrels of salt pork, haunches of frozen beef, beans, flour, molasses and sugar enough for the winter were stored away at the back of the cookhouse, under the watchful eye of the cook.

The meals were also supplemented by any wild game that was foolish enough to happen by. Because Tommy was a crack shot and could track better than any of the other men, he got time off from chopping when anyone spotted deer, moose or caribou handy to the camp.

The boys spent the winter much as they had the previous ones, swinging their axes and teaming up on the crosscut saws, "from can't see to can't see," as the older hands put it.

By late March, the spring thaw would settle in. Then the lake ice was thin and flooded and it was no longer safe to haul logs across it to the mill site. One year a team pulling an extra-big load of logs had broken through the ice near the centre of the lake and the driver and horses drowned. From then on, the company decided to err on the side of caution and shut that part of the operation down a little earlier than had been the tradition in the past.

The local farmers who had rented their teams out to the company arrived to retrieve them for the spring cultivation and planting. The horses, after a winter of hard work and good feed, were always in top condition and ready for the fields. Other horses, those that were company-owned, would stay up at the camp longer to yard the remaining felled logs to the banks of the lakes and rivers.

This particular year Danny and Tommy, being on permanent, worked later into the spring geeing and hawing their horses around the stumps, snagging the remaining logs and hauling them out of the woods. As the days grew longer, they moved down to the mill to work on sawing the logs up to make them ready for market.

In August, someone burst into the cookhouse during the evening meal and announced that England was at war with Germany. The man who brought the news was not one of the regular crew—he had signed on to operate the steam sawmill.

It was a long hard five-mile hike through the woods to the mill, so the crew stayed in the bunkhouse during the work week, but on their days off they headed home. Mr. Stevens had come up with a way to make the trip out of the woods a lot more enjoyable than the hike in.

The flume, built primarily to float lumber out, was just wide and deep enough to accommodate a crude type of narrow boat that could be thrown together in a matter of minutes at the mill site and then disassembled when it reached the millpond a half an hour later. Depending on their weight or size, three and

The Secret of the Spring

even four men could make the wild ride down the hill home in these simple craft.

On hearing the news about the war, the boys yearned to take off down the flume right away to find out what was going on with their militia, but first they had a work commitment to complete.

Danny and Tommy knew that it was only a matter of time before Canada would be involved in the war and they would be called up. It took another week for them to finish working the remaining logs into the mill and collect their pay, and during that week all the talk around the long cookhouse table and in the bunkhouse was about the war. Most of the young men were chomping at the bit and anxious to get involved, but the older men, many who had seen action during the Boer War, just sat saying nothing.

When they requested permission to leave early so they could report to their unit at Camp Aldershot, the boss, feeling it was his patriotic duty, reluctantly gave them the okay. Proud of them, though, he arranged a bit of a sendoff on their last day.

The cook put together a special meal and the celebration ran well into the night. When the crew, lighting the way with pine-pitch torches, finally escorted them to their waiting boat, Danny and Tommy saw a Union Jack made out of an old flour sack mounted on a short pole at the bow of the craft.

Someone opened the gate that controlled the flow of water into the flume a little wider than normal to hurry them on their way and when their cheering companions let the boat go, it surged forward.

Garry Leeson

Within seconds Danny and Tommy, gripping the sides of their craft, hooting with fear and delight, disappeared, flag flapping, over the brow of the hill and down into the woods.

As Danny twisted around and glanced behind him, he saw the torch light on the mountain gradually fade to nothing. They had begun their long journey into darkness.

44: What's a contingency?

Danny and Tommy hoofed it down from Rockville Notch to Kingston, found themselves a room for the night, and caught the train to Kentville the following morning. When they told the DAR conductor where they were headed, he refused payment for their tickets. There were already thirty or so other men their age, many of whom they knew, onboard. Several of them wore their militia uniforms.

When the train arrived at the Kentville station, the place was abuzz with crowds gathered to watch the recruits arrive. Shortly, a convoy of new-fangled army trucks backfired to a halt and dropped their tailgates.

The men from the train, and others who had already been waiting on the platform, tossed in their gear and climbed aboard for what was, for most of them, their first ride in a motorized vehicle that wasn't a train.

It was only a short drive to Camp Aldershot, which most of them assumed was going to be just a stopover before they headed to Halifax and boarded a troop ship. Before nightfall they had learned why the older regulars were always mumbling, "Hurry up and wait."

They spent a night at the camp, and then were

sent home the next day to put their affairs in order and say their goodbyes. For many of the men, this would be a repeat performance.

By the time they were on the train headed home, some of the realities of the situation had begun to set in. Their commanding officer had suggested that, with the help of Canada, Britain would probably be able to clean up the mess in Europe in a few short months.

"But it may take a bit longer than that," he said. "So all of you, and especially the married men, should make provision for that contingency."

"What's a contingency?" Danny whispered.

"Dunno," Tommy whispered back. "Probably something to do with being married."

The two main necessities for families of the Valley were food and heat in the winter. Since most of them lived on small, self-sufficient farms, and the men were married to capable women, they thought their families would manage with a little extra work and some careful planning. Many had done so during previous wars. They might have to slaughter and sell surplus cattle and oxen, look to the contents of their woodsheds, which the farmer-soldiers filled to capacity while they waited to be formally called up.

Danny and Tommy didn't have wives or children to worry about, but Ben wasn't getting any younger and, although the old blacksmith wouldn't admit it, he was not the man he once was. The loss of Alphonse, his best friend, had hit him hard, and he never seemed to fully recover.

The Secret of the Spring

After an evening of catching up on the local news and telling Ben, Lilly and Angie about their winter in the woods on the South Mountain, the boys hit the sack early. They were planning to head to the woodlot first thing the next morning. Something that Ben had said during dinner made what they were up to even more urgent than ever.

Ben hadn't bought the Colonel's prediction of a short war. "The man must be dreaming," he'd sputtered. "There's no such thing as a short war. Taking on Germany isn't going to be simple. You're not going up against farmers, or fellows with spears and shields. The German army...well, you'll be lucky if you're home in a couple of years, not months."

With that in mind, the boys were determined to fill the big woodshed and every other available space with as much firewood as possible before they had to leave. They spent a week felling prime hardwood. Using Ben's horse singly and teaming up their now-quiet older Sable Island ponies, they yarded thirty cords roadside.

Danny and Tommy loaded the eight-foot lengths onto the sawhorse and worked the crosscut while Ben split and loaded the finished product into the dump cart. They took load after load to the woodshed and outbuildings until they were full to bursting. The wood was still green but, with the doors left open, it would cure inside the buildings.

The same thing was happening all over the Valley. Merchants, lawyers and doctors who served as officers in the militia were hiring every local man available to stockpile fuel in the enormous sheds attached to their stately town mansions.

Mobilization didn't come all at once; there were several false starts. Every time they were summoned to the camp for training and manoeuvres they thought they might finally be on their way, but time after time that didn't happen. Many of the men had said goodbye to their wives and sweethearts so often that when they were finally really called up, it was just another quick kiss, a hug and a fare-thee-well.

45: There is a thing

1915

Ben was expecting a letter from the boys at the front, but instead the postman handed him an envelope sent from the Poor Farm in Aylesford. The letter inside concerned Skeeter Turner, a name Ben hadn't heard in years. He really hadn't known the man very well so he didn't understand why they were contacting him.

There was a note with the letter from Mr. Drew, the director of the institution. "Mr. Turner dictated the enclosed to me, and his fervent request was that I send it to you. Although he is very ill and reaching the end of his days, I should tell you that lately Mr. Turner had experienced a sort of remission from the condition that had rendered him insensible and speechless for so long. When he regained the power of speech, his first understandable words concerned this missive."

Ben put down the note and took up the letter. It was of course in the director's clear hand, but Ben heard from it an echo of the gobbling, dodging way that Skeeter used to talk.

"Ben, there is a thing. It is a thing I have to tell you before I pass. I have it clear in my head but I am afraid soon I will lose my chance to get it out right.

They want me to tell it to the master so he can write it here, but I cannot. I cannot. I must tell it to only you. No good thing came out of my life so far, but maybe if I tell you this that may be one. So come soon. You don't have to be afraid to come, as these people are kindly. But come soon, before I am gone."

The next day, thinking that he was probably setting out on a fool's errand, Ben hitched his old horse to the light buggy, kissed Lilly goodbye and set off down the Valley toward Aylesford. It was a beautiful spring day and, at seventy-eight years of age, Ben considered that he deserved a little time away from the forge now and then. He still had his health, he could still swing a hammer, and he could still be a husband to his wife but, all the same, a little holiday would be welcome.

He knew the way to the Poor Farm; it was situated very close to old Camp Aldershot, the last place he was stationed in the military. He only stopped once along the way. In the village of Kingston, he found water for his horse in a trough by the train station and treated himself to a chunk of cheese and a handful of crackers out of the barrel in the general store.

Trotting at a leisurely pace, it didn't take long to reach the Glebe Road, where Camp Aldershot had been. It had moved over to Kentville about ten years earlier, and all that was left was scrub brush struggling on the desert-like sand. Nature, as is its way, was busy erasing history.

He pushed on, crossed the Annapolis River through a short covered bridge, and took the turn

The Secret of the Spring

that would lead him to the Poor Farm Road. Half a mile on, the buildings came into view.

There was a huge, three-story wooden structure that was obviously for housing, with barns and outbuildings scattered around it. The nearer fields were all planted in vegetables and there were about fifty men all dressed in grey strung along straight rows of green seedlings, scraping the earth with their hoes. When they stopped and leaned on their implements to watch him pass, they looked just like the scarecrows that had been erected in the field.

The lawn in front of the main building was shaded by two huge elms. Some residents who were ambulatory but too weak, sick, or crazy to help in the fields were gathered in their shade.

Ben pulled up to a hitching rail and climbed out of the buggy, but before he could tie his horse, a wave of people came running over, crowding around and pawing at him.

"Now, now," he said, pushing them aside as gently as he could.

"Nah nah," a toothless man responded.

Then others took up the chorus. "Nah nah. Nah nah," they murmured as they trailed after Ben as he moved toward the main entrance.

"You got candy?" a teenage girl asked. "You got candy?" She fluttered her eyes at him. "Candy?"

Two young boys, who were tied by long ropes to the elm trees, had come to the end of their tethers and were reaching toward him with pleading looks on their faces. He could not fathom what they could hope he had for them.

Suddenly the front door to the building opened and a well-dressed older man took a step forward. As he did, the mob fell silent and, like beaten animals, started to shuffle away.

"They mean you no harm," the man said. "Please step in. My name is Drew."

Ben wondered at the sort of treatment the inmates must endure to elicit the reaction he had just witnessed. Lilly had asked if she could make the trip with him, and now he thanked God that he had had the foresight to spare her this.

Enos Drew had been in charge of the institution for over ten years and had become immune to the madness that surrounded him. As he led Ben through the building and up several flights of stairs, he felt no need to explain the bizarre sights and situations they encountered.

There was only one exception. As they drew near to the door of a ward, the director paused and touched Ben's arm lightly. "If you give a wide birth to our brother here, it will be easier on him and perhaps on yourself."

The man in question crouched against the wall, naked except for the shackle and chain that secured him to an iron radiator. He was shivering, not from cold, but as if a current stronger than his body could control was running through him.

Ben followed Mr. Drew into a long, narrow room. They made their way along a central corridor that

The Secret of the Spring

separated the footboards of a dozen or more white iron beds whose headboards were flat against the walls. The air was heavy with the stench of urine and feces. Ben instinctively reached for his handkerchief, then thought better of it and left it in his pocket.

Skeeter's cot was in a far corner of the room. The object that occupied it no longer looked human. He was a yellowed, brittle husk of skin wrapped tightly around a skeleton.

At first Ben thought he was looking at a corpse and that he had come too late. But as they drew close to the bed, Skeeter inhaled a raspy breath and his eyes opened.

"Good: he is awake," Mr. Drew said. "Skeeter, you have your visitor."

Skeeter's lips moved silently.

"Yes, well. I will leave you to your visit," Mr. Drew said to Ben. "If there is need, pray ring that bell and an attendant will come."

Ben watched the man leave, then turned his attention to Skeeter. He bent forward and said softly, "Hello. You wrote to me and here I am."

"Is he gone?" the faint voice creaked.

"We are alone."

"Alphonse."

Ben felt a chill run down his spine, and had to force himself to speak calmly. "He was my friend. What of him?"

The story tumbled out of how Alphonse had met his end. Ben struggled to lean in close enough to catch Skeeter's every word, for his whole self wanted to move as far as he could from this frail man and his foul tale. But he had to know.

And as Ben listened, anger such as he hadn't felt in years took possession of him. This was no fancy of a deluded, dying man. Every detail rang clearly, even in the garbled and tangled telling.

At last the faint voice ceased and Skeeter was done. Exhausted, he stared up at Ben as if hoping for some reward, perhaps forgiveness or absolution. Or perhaps, like the girl outside, for a piece of candy.

Ben turned and walked away. If he had stayed he might have been tempted to smash what was left of the old man's frail body to smithereens.

46: Bash, bash

On the trip home Ben tried to shake the demon that he thought he had left behind on the battlefields and in the London of his youth. But it had hold of him with a grip he had never felt before.

Pete Zink, Pete Zink! It screamed over and over in his mind.

By the time he was in sight of home he knew what he was going to do. His horse tried to turn into the familiar dooryard as they approached but he yanked the off rein and made him continue down the road in the direction of the spring.

His anger had blinded him to the fact he was an old man now, and that Pete Zink was a huge man in the prime of life who for years had crippled and maimed anyone foolish enough to tangle with him. His demon had never allowed for these kinds of considerations in the past and it didn't now. He just hoped Pete was still at his shack by the spring.

There was no need to go further up the mountain. As Ben approached the copse of pines that shaded the spring, he saw the big man standing close to the water, holding a yoke with water pails suspended on either end.

Pete turned and watched while Ben turned the buggy off the road and climbed stiffly down to tie his horse to a tree. He gave Ben a long look of disdain, then turned away. He took his pails off the yoke and knelt to dip the first one into the spring. That's when he heard Ben's quiet deliberate voice.

"Get to your feet, you bastard."

"What did you say?" Pete shot back, immediately aroused and angry. Then, remembering that he had just been released from the Kings County Jail the day before and was on parole, he decided to let the insult slide.

"I said, 'get to your feet, you bastard,' and do it now!"

"Go away, old man. You're bothering me." Pete turned back to fussing with his pails.

Seconds passed and he didn't hear the old man leaving. Pete looked over his shoulder and saw Ben remove his jacket.

He got to his feet and turned to face him. "What the hell is on your mind, you old fool? What do you think you're going to do?"

"I plan to kill you, Peter Zink, but first I plan to hurt you the way you hurt my friend."

"What did I do to any friend of yours?"

"You tied him to that railroad track."

Pete guffawed. "So *that*'s what this is all about, a fucking, no-good Frenchie. Hell, the only good ones are dead ones. Piss off."

With that, fists clenched, Ben started for him.

Pete was ready—he still had the yoke in his hand behind his back, and as Ben swung for him, he lashed out with the heavy oak stick, striking Ben a crippling blow to his left shoulder.

Ben staggered backwards, but kept to his feet. He bobbed and ducked as Pete continued toward him, swinging his cudgel.

Ben was in pain, but he wasn't afraid. His mind was busy with cold calculation. He was waiting for Pete to make the one mistake that would allow him to release the fury he had carried with him from Skeeter's bedside.

His moment came when Pete's foot caught briefly on an exposed root and the big man looked down for a split second.

As he looked up again, Ben swung his left fist at him as a feint. When Pete went to block it, Ben sent his right one forward into the surprised man's face with all the strength he could muster.

Ben felt the crunch of bones as Pete's nose flattened against his face. He took half a step backward and brought his knee sharply up into Pete's groin, causing him to drop his stick.

Ben knew from past experience that if he took advantage of his opponent's confusion and used the flat of his hand as a weapon to drive the shards of broken nose bone up and into Pete's brain he would die instantly, but that would have been letting him off too easy. Instead he took his time, inviting the clumsy giant to come at him, then hammering his face and body with a series of lightning-fast punches. With each blow he said, "Alphonse."

In no time, Pete's face was a bloody pulp and he

was unable to see. Ben kicked the man's legs out from under him and, as he lay on the ground moaning and pleading, drove his heavy-booted foot into his testicles. He kicked Pete in the same spot over and over, until the big man was motionless and unresponsive.

Thinking to revive him so he could resume the punishment, Ben dragged Pete's heavy, limp body to the spring and thrust him head-first into the icy waters.

Then the pain struck him.

At first he thought it was in the left shoulder, where Pete had hit him with the yoke. But the pain became more intense.

Ben looked down past the struggling man beneath him and into the waters of the spring. His vision began to blur and swirl and suddenly he became very dizzy.

As he fainted, the full weight of his body fell on the half-submerged Pete Zink and held him in place until the last bubbles of the man's breath broke the surface and his body was still.

When Ben came to an hour later, it was dark and the moon was reflecting off the still surface of the spring. He knew the man beneath him was dead.

Shuddering in disgust, Ben rolled off him and tried to get to his feet, but something was wrong. His left arm was numb and wouldn't take his weight when he tried to hoist himself up. Using the other arm, he finally got to his feet, only to find that his left leg was useless, too. It was numb. He could put a bit

The Secret of the Spring

of his weight on it, but when he tried to take a step, it collapsed beneath him and he fell down.

He could see the wooden yoke lying few feet away. If he could get to it, he could use it as a crutch.

After another unsuccessful attempt to stand, he gave up and crawled, dragging himself over the ground. It was only a small distance but he found himself short of breath and barely made it.

He rested a while, and then, supporting himself with the yoke, he got to his feet and moved slowly over to his horse. Discarding his crutch, he untied the animal, leaned on its flanks, and inched his way back along the shafts to the big front wheel of the carriage.

After yet another rest to catch his breath he slowly hauled himself up to the seat where he plopped down. He swung his useless arm over the back of the seat to hold himself upright.

The reins were lying slackly over the dashboard and he reached forward with his right hand and grabbed them. Pulling back on them, he spoke to the horse. He tried to say, "Back, Back," but his words came out, "Bash, Bash,' and he realized that, although Pete had never hit it, one side of his face was strangely numb and slack.

The horse responded anyway, backing away from the tree, so Ben dropped the reins and swung his good arm over the back of the seat as well. He sat with his arms pinioned in that fashion for a few seconds until he managed to say, "Gish Shup," to the horse, who had turned his head back and was looking past his blinkers at him. The horse responded and moved off slowly.

Ben's head slumped backwards. He sat in that position with his feet pushed firmly against the dashboard and let the old horse make his own way home.

The horse was in no hurry—he hadn't been fed all day and as he slowly made his way along the road in the direction of the smithy, he stopped frequently to graze on tufts of grass at the edge of the ditches.

Lilly and Angie were sitting at the kitchen table when they heard the buggy rattle into the yard. "Finally!" Lilly said as she pushed her chair back and got to her feet.

She left Angie sitting at the table while she headed out the door, preparing to give Ben a piece of her mind for being so late and making her worry.

"Ben! What have you been about so long?"

He didn't answer. She grabbed the hurricane lantern that hung on the veranda post and held it high as she walked toward the buggy.

Finally she could see him clearly. Ben was sitting rigidly still, with his eyes staring defiantly past her at something, she knew not what.

"Where is your coat, you foolish man? You'll catch your death!"

They buried Ben up on the mountain beside his old friend Alphonse.

47: In slow time: move out!

When the gas warning gong began to sound, Tommy was on watch and had plenty of time to get his gas mask. But he was worried about Danny, who was asleep in the dugout, so he hurried down to him. He was almost in time.

Danny got a whiff of the chlorine gas but, with Tommy's help, he got his gas mask in place so it wasn't as terrible as it could have been.

Danny tried to tell the medical officer it was just the cold he had been struggling with over the past week that was causing his coughing and gagging but the officer wouldn't listen. He pointed to the long line of soldiers with bandages over their eyes who were ready to march away from the front.

"You may not be able to breathe much, but at least you can see. Go to the front of the line, Private."

Once Danny was in place, the officer said, "Right: invalided file: place your hand on the shoulder of the man in front of you." He had to raise his voice over the rattle of German machine-gun fire and the thuds of exploding shells.

As soon as the men had themselves organized, the officer shouted, "Column, in slow time: move out!"

The men staggered along through the ankle-deep mud. Danny kept swinging around to check on those behind them, and frequently had to signal the officer in charge to call a halt so he could go back and help those whose hand had slipped from the man ahead, or had tripped. They had to leave some of the fallen to wait for the stretcher bearers who trailed the column.

His chest felt like a small campfire was burning away in it. *At least I have my eyes*, he kept repeating to himself.

When they reached the narrow-gauge railway that would carry them away from the front, Danny once again tried to plead his case. "I'm all right, sir. Please let me go back to the regiment."

"You don't sound all right. Get your ass on that train."

When they arrived at a damaged chateau that was serving as a field hospital, Danny tried again to find someone who would clear him for duty. Since he could not get three words out before a coughing fit overtook him, no one would take him seriously. His status was as a patient for now.

As long as he moved slowly and didn't try to speak, he didn't really feel all that bad, so he made himself busy helping the nurses and orderlies attend to those who were really in need.

A new officer arrived to oversee the evacuation of the patients back to old Blighty. When he saw Danny moving about the ward, he cast a suspicious eye on him and asked the matron, "Is he another one claiming battle fatigue, or just good, old-fashioned cowardice?"

The Secret of the Spring

"No cowardice in him," matron said. "He would be back on the lines today if anybody would let him go."

"And why don't they? We're short of men."

Matron fixed him with a hard look. "He is sicker than you or he thinks. If you send him back now, he won't last long enough for a bullet to find him."

~

It was a full month before a captain from his own regiment appeared and stopped Danny to ask how he was. Danny renewed his plea to return to active duty. By now, if he chose carefully when to breathe and how long a sentence to embark on, he could keep the coughing under control.

"I don't know why you're so anxious to get back to that hell hole," the captain finally said, "but if you must, get on your way."

Danny hoofed it without a backward glance!

It wasn't difficult to find his way back to the front. All he had to do was head toward the sound of the artillery. But as he trudged along, the barrage seemed to be intensifying.

Soon he began to see the results. Frequently he had to scramble off the muddy track to allow supply trucks to pass or make way for the four-horse teams galloping in front of the caissons hauling the huge spools of cable wire for the signal corps.

He had come abreast of an improvised veterinary clinic when one single pistol shot drew his attention. Shielded by a huge ancient rock wall, a long string of sad, wounded horses were waiting their turn. The shot he had heard was the quickest method of ending the pain the animals were enduring.

At that moment a huge Krupp shell exploded on the road ahead of him, knocking him to the ground. Then, through the cloud of dust and debris, three panicked horses came stampeding toward him. He just had time to roll to one side to escape being trampled.

When the air cleared a bit, Danny made his way forward. Above the steaming shell crater the severed front quarter of a horse was dangling high in the crotch of a shattered tree, dripping blood and staring down accusingly at him.

He made his way through a sea of carnage, both animal and human, until he reached the relative safety of the trench he and Tommy had helped dig. He walked over the duckboards until he came to their dugout. He and Tommy always felt secure sleeping in their bunker. Two of the Cape Breton men they shared it with had used their coal-mining skills to help them build it.

"Look who's back," one of the men inside said as he parted the blanket and stuck his head in.

"Where's Tommy?"

"Don't worry, Danny boy. He'll be back shortly. He got himself into a bit of trouble a couple of days after you left and he's been busy paying the piper. I think this is the last day of his crucifixion."

"His what?" Danny stammered

"His crucifixion. You know, Field Punishment

Number One. Tommy has been standing handcuffed to a big cart wheel three hours a day ever since you left."

"What the hell did he do to deserve that?"

"Drunk and disorderly."

"What are you talking about? Tommy doesn't drink?"

One of the older men said, "Maybe he didn't, but he sure does now. He's been trading everything he can get his hands on for extra rum rations."

"But disorderly?"

"When he got his own ration at stand-to that morning, he'd already had more than a snoot full. He was slow doing his practice climb up his attack ladder and the sergeant goosed him. Tommy took a swing at him before falling into the mud."

"Crucifixion ain't so bad," the first man said. "It's lot better than the floggings they used to do."

Danny decided to wait for Tommy further down along the trench. He didn't have to wait long.

"Danny! I thought you were never coming back. Nobody seemed to know anything about you. I thought maybe you'd bought it and I was going to have to write Aunt Lilly and Mom."

Danny decided that he would not confront Tommy with what he'd just heard. Having grown up in the shadow of Ben and Alphonse—one who had never touched the stuff and the other who fought to resist the hold it had on him—he still found the attraction of strong drink a mystery. He just said, "Have there been any letters from home?"

The next morning at stand-to, Danny offered his rum ration to Tommy. Tommy added it to his mug but passed both quarter gills over to the next man in line. "I guess you forgot," he said, straight-faced. "I never touch the stuff."

48: You make of it what you will

A ground fog had settled over No Man's Land. It was a welcome gift to the men who would shortly ascend their ladders and fling themselves into a maelstrom of rifle and machine-gun fire. The German mortars were already in full swing and the Allied artillery was responding in kind.

The regiment would attack two men short. Tommy and Danny were already huddled in a huge bomb crater close to the German lines. Just before midnight they had slid cautiously over the lip of their trench and snaked their way through the maze of shell holes and tangled wire. As they inched along, they would freeze motionless when the German flares lit up the area. Rotting corpses from both sides lay strewn everywhere around them and, to a German sniper's quick glance, the very still Tommy and Danny would be indistinguishable.

Just before they made it to the relative safety of a crater, a number of huge rats clustered on a cadaver nearby made the body appear to be moving. A Maxim machine gun fired a short burst, exploding the body and killing some of the rats but narrowly missing Tommy and Danny.

It was a close call, but now they knew where the pill box was. That was why they were out on the patrol.

The Captain's orders had been brief. "Locate that machine gun that has been doing us so much harm. The artillery fellas will make short work of it once they know where it is. And, Tommy: if the opportunity presents itself, I wouldn't mind if you used that new Lee-Enfield to take out that gunner—he's done in enough of our Canadian men."

"Yessir."

"Get that done and get that info back as soon as you can. If you do a good job, you can stand down when you get back and leave the rest to the others."

The Captain checked his watch. "Small red flares will go up on the hour: one for one o'clock, two for two o'clock, and so on. The assault is scheduled for sunrise but get yourselves back well before then."

"If we get back before two," Danny said, "that will save two flares."

The Captain gave him a tight smile. "War on a shoestring: good thinking."

Tommy was the best shot in the regiment, so he was the natural pick for the recon. Danny had volunteered to go with him.

The Secret of the Spring

Now, wearing black balaclavas instead of helmets and their faces blackened, they were hunkered down, knee-deep in putrid water, when they saw the single red flare.

Tommy whispered closely into Danny's ear, "Those stupid bastards are smoking in the pill box. The next time I see the glow of a cigarette tip, I'll finish that gunner. Then we better get our asses out of here."

The German flares lit up a fairly straight escape path back to their trenches and they decided that they would chance an exposed, full-out run back home when the time came. There would be confusion in the pill box and that should give them enough time.

The opportunity presented itself just as the two red flares appeared above their line. Danny's shot was followed by a horrible scream from the pill box.

"Now!" Tommy barked. "We go now!"

Danny started clambering up the side of the shell hole, but suddenly stopped when he heard a low voice saying, "Stay put! Get down and stay put."

"Did you hear that, Tommy?"

"Hear what? Are you crazy? Get out of my way! I'm outta here."

At that moment all hell broke out. The rolling barrage that had been planned for sunrise started up hours early. Their escape route was blown to smithereens and heavy British shells were landing and exploding all around them.

The generals had seized on an early opportunity. Danny and Tommy were rendered expendable.

They woke up from that endless, deafening night surprised to be alive, being carried on stretchers to the field hospital.

~

Danny and Tommy were transported together across the Channel but when they arrived in England, they ended up in different hospitals according to their individual injuries. They weren't to see each other for a full six weeks.

By then, Danny was fully recovered; but Tommy's neck injury was serious and would need a lot more time to heal. Danny only had a little time before he had to ship out and rejoin his regiment but something had happened that he needed to share with Tommy.

After some heartfelt sympathy for his suffering friend, Danny pulled a letter from his pocket and got around to the real purpose of his visit. "I got this letter from Ma two days ago. It isn't good news, Tommy. My Dad has died. Old Ben is gone."

"Oh, Danny, I'm so sorry. You know I loved him as much as you did. How did he die? What caused it?"

"Her letter isn't so clear about that, but here is something I need you to see."

Danny unfolded the copy of a death certificate that had been included with the letter. "Look at the date and time of death that Doctor Rutledge filled in."

"Yeah, I see it: 9 pm, Wednesday, April 15."

"Ring any bells, Tommy?"

"What do you mean?"

"Think back to the night that got us into this mess. Do you remember what time it was when the barrage started?"

"How could I ever forget that? Two red flares up: 2 am."

"And why did we get lucky and stay in that shell hole?"

"You mean the voice you said you heard telling us to stay put?"

"Right. When I read this paper, it hit me. I heard that voice at 2 am on Thursday and Ben died at home at 9 pm on Wednesday."

"And so..?"

"Don't you see? 2 am in Belgium on Thursday is the exact same time as 9 pm on Wednesday in Nova Scotia!"

"Are you trying to tell me that that voice—?"

"I'm not trying to tell you anything, Tommy. You make of it what you will and I'll believe what I believe. I gotta go, or I'll miss my train."

49: You look a treat

1916

Tommy Arseneau sat opening the latest package from home. On top was a letter for him from his Mum. Aunt Lilly usually did the writing for Angie, who wasn't as comfortable writing herself, so the letters ended up a mixture of both Angie's and Lilly's thoughts.

Things were not going particularly well back home now that Ben had died, but the two women made light of their circumstances. He lifted a pair of thick woollen socks out of the parcel and, as he pressed them to his face, he could almost see the two women knitting outside on the veranda in the afternoon and then by the cookstove in the evening. He could even detect a faint smell of the wood smoke that meant home to him.

As always when these offerings from home made it to the convalescent hospital where he was recuperating from his neck wound, he would find practical clothing, stale but edible cookies and as many safely-packed jars of preserves as the box would hold. This time they had included a brightly-coloured handkerchief like the ones he and Danny had worn around their necks in their lumberjack days; a little large, but all lovingly hand-stitched.

He didn't know why they had sent it. Maybe they thought he would like something to wear around his neck to hide his hideous wound, or maybe it was just a bit of colour to cheer him up.

He tied it on and then went to the window where he could see his reflection. What he saw pleased him—the bright-red bandana glowed in stark contrast to the drab, off-white hospital clothing.

When he looked through the window beyond his own wispy image, across the lawns of the great house that now served as a hospital, he could see the streets of a village spread out below him. Something unusual was happening. The normally quiet square was crammed with people and long lines of horses were tethered around the perimeter.

It was a horse fair. He knew they had them every year, but last year he had been too ill to attend. Now he was still having the odd dizzy spell, but he thought a bit of a walk might do him good. He hadn't had his hand on a horse for a long time, not since he'd left the front. It would be nice to see some animals that weren't terrified and constantly flinching at the sound of exploding artillery shells.

"Just the thing," the ward nurse said when Tommy announced his intention. "I would go myself, if they let me off. Say hello to the horses for me."

The attending military surgeon had pronounced that he would soon be fit enough to return to active duty with his battalion. He just needed to recover his physical strength so a trip down the hill to the village would do him good.

The Secret of the Spring

The nurse found him some civilian trousers and a soft, checkered shirt from the supply of used clothing that the local ladies' auxiliary had provided for the patients. "You look a treat," she said. "Every maiden's fondest dream."

Tommy bathed and shaved and pulled on his borrowed clothes. As he stood in front of the bathroom mirror, tying his new neckerchief and brushing his jet black hair, he realized how long it had grown. He was certainly in need of a haircut, but they would shave it off before he headed back to the front anyway. No need to bother about it for now.

He pulled on his army issue boots and headed down the hill toward the village, enjoying a school-holiday feeling.

The smell of horse sweat and fresh manure greeted him long before he reached the square. After the smell of ether and antiseptic he'd been living with, it was like an old friend to him.

He made his way along the lines of horses, mentally assessing them. He knew if he showed too much interest in any one mount, its owner would assail him with a speech about the beast's fine properties and the promise of a bargain price if Tommy was minded to buy it.

Scattered throughout the crowd were dark-complexioned men in colourful attire adorned with beads, and glinting earrings. These were the gypsies, or 'Roma', he had heard of but never seen.

He watched, fascinated, as they worked the

crowd. Sidling over and leaning in close, he listened to their pitches as they bought, sold and traded.

A dozen ornately-painted caravans were lined up on one of the roads leading into the square and Tommy was tempted to go and have a closer look at them, but after walking the horse lines several times he decided that he should find a place to sit down to rest a bit. He had thought himself fit but his first venture abroad was leaving him a little tired. He could also feel a slight headache and that was usually a precursor to one of his dizzy spells.

The two local pubs were full to capacity, but the enterprising owners had erected trestle tables outside. Tommy found an empty chair at the first establishment he came to. He sat down and ordered a pint.

He never finished it. The world began to swirl and then he blacked out and slumped forward onto the table. His mug fell from his hand and smashed on the cobbles.

When he came to, he thought he was in a field ambulance. There was a curved roof above him and the vehicle seemed to be in motion.

He sat up and had a closer look around. Field ambulances weren't decorated with painted flowers. They didn't have stoves and cupboards, rugs and plush curtains. He was in a gypsy caravan!

He got up and peered out the rear door. The town and the hospital were nowhere in sight.

How the hell did I end up here? he thought. *Have I been kidnapped?*

The Secret of the Spring

Then an older man, one of the traders he had seen, climbed up the back steps into the wagon. "Ah, you're back with us," he said with real concern in his voice.

"What the hell is going on? Where am I?"

"Now settle down. You're with your people. You're safe now." The old gypsy patted Tommy's hand. "We're on the move, just putting some distance between us and the fellas we sold some 'young' horses to!"

Tommy suddenly realized that they had taken him for a Roma because of his colouring and his attire. He wanted to laugh, but thought better of it. It was already dark and he had no idea what time it was. He was already AWOL and this was certainly more interesting than hospital life.

One by one the wagons made their way through a gate in a stone wall and drew into a circle. The men unhitched the horses and turned them out to graze.

Tommy watched as they lit a large fire in the centre of the encampment and women in long, colourful dresses scurried around with baskets and cooking pots. Several of the men appeared with guitars and mandolins and struck up a tune. The women started to sway to the rhythm while they cooked, as if fighting the urge to dance.

Tommy had never seen anything like it; it was magical.

Tommy planned to return to the hospital in the morning, but he never did. He stayed with these strange, welcoming people. He saw in the Roma the same free-spirited life he had experienced as a youngster with his parents, as they plied the tinker's trade with their old horse and cart on their way up the Valley to rejoin Ben, Angie and Danny.

He knew he would be a deserter if he didn't go back, and he knew the consequences if he were apprehended. But perhaps the army and the local constabulary wouldn't look too hard for him. Too many depressed and traumatized survivors of the trenches had wandered off. Sometimes people found them hanging by the neck in remote barns or floating bloated in the rivers and canals. *Perhaps I can claim I have lost my memory...*

Once the caravans moved further north and Tommy felt it was safe, he wrote to his mother about his new circumstances, so she would not worry if some official message from the War Department arrived at her door.

Roma have no fixed address, but he knew where she was and wrote at least a line every few weeks. And once in a while a loving response found its way to him.

The story became that, in the years after the Great War, one particular Roma family always had a special welcome among the heavily-wooded northern estates in Yorkshire. The gypsy man was incredibly handy with the axe, the saw and the shaving bench. And he had a remarkable way with young colts and the more spirited horses that most men could not manage.

50: No parade

March, 1919

The area around the railway station in Middleton was crowded with hundreds of people waiting for the Flying Bluenose to arrive. The long, brown-shingled building with its warehouse and waiting room was draped in red, white and blue bunting, and flapping Union Jacks hung from the telegraph wires. The local band had been playing lively tunes for over an hour and all present were smiling excitedly and in the mood for a party.

There was a great deal of back slapping and bragging as several jugs passed discretely among the men who waited near the rear of the throng. The war had ended on the eleventh hour of the eleventh day, four months earlier, and today's train was bringing the first of the boys home.

Lilly and Angie didn't go to town. They had no reason to, for their boys weren't coming home.

Lilly's son, Danny, had written to say his return would be delayed because, for some unexplained reason, he had been sent to Russia with several other local men who were serving with his regiment. Angie's son, Tommy, would not be coming home, either. The last official news she had received was that he was missing, not the dreaded missing-in-action notice, simply missing. She was relieved she now knew otherwise, by a message from Tommy that had arrived around Thanksgiving.

It was for the best that the two women had chosen to stay at home, because the homecoming was not at all what the people of the area had expected. The first men to come home weren't the strutting heroes; instead, they were the injured and wounded.

The excitement and jubilation of the crowd had reached a frenzied pitch as the train roared into the station with the band playing "Rule Britannia" and everyone shouting and cheering. When nurses and orderlies began to help the boys they knew off the train, a hush came over the crowd and the music dwindled away.

Some of the men were on crutches and some were lifted to the station platform by burly, uniformed men, while they clutched the arms of their wheelchairs. There were missing hands, legs and arms—two were blind and many had terrible disfiguring facial scars.

Even those men who appeared whole and uninjured were barely recognizable—ghostly facsimiles of the robust, laughing young recruits who'd left the station a few years before.

After their initial shock, the waiting relatives rushed forward to embrace their sons, brothers and fathers. The town band reluctantly struck up with the lively march they had planned on playing during

The Secret of the Spring

a victory parade up Main Street, but after one stanza they lost heart and stopped.

There would be no parade, not on that day.

Most of the crowd had already started to leave by the time the last of the soldiers were disembarking. Many of the townsfolk had immediately turned away when the first of the injured appeared because they were embarrassed, uneasy and didn't know what to say or do.

The train moved on, the injured warriors were helped into waiting buggies and farm wagons, and in the space of an hour, only three uniformed men were still left sitting on the benches, drinking tea and munching on the neat little sandwiches the Baptist church ladies had provided.

Lilly's brother, Darrell, balancing a plate of food on his lap and holding a mug of tea in his one remaining hand, watched as an apologetic, tardy brother collected one of his brothers-in-arms. Shortly after, the only other man wandered off on foot, mumbling something about a 'damned no good wife!'

Darrell had expected his father or brother to come for him, but after sitting on the bench for an additional hour, he figured he'd better start hoofing it up the mountain.

He was all right for the first mile or so, but then he started feeling short of breath and very, very hot. He hadn't felt this weak since they had first amputated part of his arm and it had become infected. He knew it wasn't the arm that was troubling him now—the stump was still itchy but it wasn't feverish or painful.

Whatever was coming over him was coming on fast, and as he trudged on, he became dizzy and his head started throbbing. He was on his last legs when he turned a corner and the blacksmith shop came into view. He somehow found enough strength to stagger the remaining distance to his sister's house before collapsing in her dooryard.

Angie was the first to see the khaki-clad figure lying face down in the gravel in front of the house. She put her pail of milk down, rushed over and knelt beside him, visions of her Tommy flashing through her mind.

When she rolled the moaning man over and saw who he was, she was shocked and uncertain what to do. Lilly's father and brothers had never been allowed on the property.

Then Lilly came to stand beside her. She stood staring in disbelief for a short time and then, with a look of resignation, said, "Give me a hand. Let's get him into the house."

In addition to the medals and souvenirs the boys had acquired on the battlefields of Europe, they had also unknowingly brought home a deadly virus. The Spanish Flu had arrived.

"Angie, take the horse and buggy and fetch the doctor," Lilly said. "I'll try to do something to keep him comfortable."

There was nothing on hand to deal with such a

fever. She sat beside Darrell, bathing his brow and listening to his laboured breathing.

Then Angie was back, alone. "The doctor can't come. Lots of the soldiers that came back are sick, just like this. He's says he'll get to us when he can."

As it turned out, the doctor's visit wasn't necessary for two days later Lilly's brother was dead.

Dreading the idea of having to see her father again, Lilly sent word asking him to come and pick Darrell's body up so he could be buried in the Leonard plot up on the mountain. Later that day, leaving the unpleasant task to Angie, she stayed in the barn while her inebriated father and remaining brother, Gordie, took the corpse away in their rickety wagon.

51: Pretty far-fetched

In all the years that Lilly and Angie had been friends they had never had a serious argument. But they were having words now, strong words. Angie was berating her.

"You owe it to the boy. He needs to know. It's what Ben would have wanted. Ben was always saying how sorry he was that he didn't know who his own father was. That boy of yours went away thinking one of your crazy brothers was his father and that he was some kind of freak."

They were rereading the letters they had received from the boys during the war and one of the letters that Danny had written had started it all. It seemed that somehow they had missed seeing a newspaper clipping that he had enclosed.

Before starting to read the letter aloud, Lilly unfolded the yellowing newsprint. She suddenly gasped, leapt to her feet and turned her head away. She felt herself drifting away to a place she hadn't visited since she was a young girl.

"What is it?" Angie said. She flew around the table to Lilly's side. Lilly was staring off at nothing, as if hypnotized.

Angie picked up the bit of torn newspaper that had so startled Lilly. The heading read 'King George

Visits His Troops on the Western Front.' Scribbled below was a note in pencil: "Guess what, Mum? The King talked to me and shook my hand."

The picture beside the article was of the King inspecting a group of soldiers. A pencilled line lead from the note to Danny standing in the front row.

"Oh, Lilly," Angie said. She immediately knew what had caused Lilly's reaction. "Tell me, tell me what you're thinking."

Lilly just stared into space, unresponsive.

Angie spoke to her softly, then sharply, with no response. Finally, she stepped forward and slapped her friend's face.

Lilly shook her head, turned to Angie, and started to sob. "Oh, I had forgotten that it happened. I swear to God that if you had told me yesterday, I would have said you were crazy. But it did happen, didn't it?"

"It happened, Lil. And now I think it's time you dealt with it. Long past time. Ben went to the grave thinking that Danny's father was one of your brothers, but you and I know that that was never the whole story. You need to tell Danny the truth—"

"I can't!"

"—because, and this may be news to you, he already knows that Ben isn't his real father."

Lilly gasped. Her sobbing stopped.

"Did you really think a secret like that would be safe in a place like this?" Angie continued. "I didn't tell you at the time because I didn't want to upset you and I didn't know what Ben might do, but my

Tommy told me how they found out. They were around fourteen."

"Just children..."

"They were in town on a Saturday night, standing in front of the general store hoping some girls would pass by. They heard some sort of kerfuffle going on in the store and then a body came flying out the door. The man landed face down on the planking, hitting his head and knocking himself out. It was your brother Harold. He was drunk and stealing and the store keeper had ejected him. Then the store keeper turned to Danny and said, 'Get your uncle, or maybe your father, the hell out of here!'"

Lilly buried her face in her hands, but Angie could tell she was listening. "The boys weren't long finding out what everybody supposed was the whole story. But, Lil, you and I know that that isn't the real story. The real story isn't nice, but it's a hell of a lot better than what he believes now. Isn't it better to be known as the bastard son of a King than of an inbred idiot? By God, Lilly, if you don't tell him, I will!"

Lilly had nothing to say. She knew Angie was right. "I'll write a letter," she said. "I won't send it now. I'll wait until he's home safe. I don't want him upset while he's still away. He might get angry and never come home."

She broke into tears and Angie took her in her arms and hugged her.

As good as her word, Lilly wrote the letter the next day. She was tempted to sugarcoat her words, but she realized that there was really no way of

The Secret of the Spring

doing that, so she told him the truth, leaving nothing out.

After letting Angie read it, she said, "You know, putting it down in writing like that, it seems pretty far-fetched. Do you suppose he'll believe me?"

"He'll believe you. And if he doesn't, you'll always have me to back you up."

Lilly went to the bureau and got the little red cake tin where she kept her special things, folded the letter, slipped it in and closed the lid. It was ready to send or give to him when the time was right.

That time never came, though. Two weeks later Lilly became ill with the same symptoms her brother had shown. Despite everything her friend tried to do to save her, she died two weeks after that.

Not even the miraculous waters of the spring seemed to help.

Garry Leeson

52: Shades of Russia

Toronto, Ontario
August 16 1933

Police Constable Daniel Johnson was not a happy man. He sat on his horse on Pembroke Street, in the company of twelve other officers, waiting for orders to advance into Toronto's Allen Gardens. Thousands of unemployed workers, many of them vets like himself, were peacefully protesting, trying to get some recognition from a government that didn't seem to care.

Chief Constable Draper was mounted as well, and that always meant trouble. He was an old warhorse who had commanded the 5th Canadian Rifles during the war. A strict disciplinarian, he'd been recruited to bring order to a burgeoning city that was starting to show signs of revolution.

Danny had been with Draper and his mounted unit when they broke up the Communist rallies at Queen's Park and had earned the nickname, Draper's Dragoons. He wasn't proud of what they had been forced to do when the crowd in front of the provincial parliament buildings had refused to disperse.

That was different from what was expected of them today. Agitators in that crowd had initiated the violence and he and the other mounted officers simply responded in kind. Today he would be facing old comrades, men who had been in the trenches beside him and, like him, probably still woke in the middle of the night in cold sweats, remembering the horrors of war.

What will I say to Margaret when I get home?

It was different when he was at Queen's Park. Both he and Margaret knew firsthand about communism and realized that the people who were promoting and advocating it were misguided. They had met in Russia when he was there on a hushed-up mission after the war ended. She was serving as a nurse at a temporary hospital in Murmansk. They had witnessed how the best-laid plans of men like Lenin and Trotsky went awry and got twisted into an unworkable, abusive system.

Neither of them was about to apologize for the part Danny played in slowing that movement down, but the demonstration today was a different matter.

As he watched the crowds gathering in the distance and caught the odd glimpse of partial khaki uniforms scattered throughout, he wondered, *What the hell am I doing here?* If Margaret's father hadn't been a police inspector and high up in the Orange Lodge, he would probably be up there in the park begging for justice with the rest of those vets.

There, but for the grace of God, go I. He remembered his father's stories of the veterans from the charge at Balaclava who had ended their lives in London's workhouses.

To Danny's relief, the mounted unit was held in

reserve that day. Instead, two hundred regular officers advanced to disperse the crowd. They were having very little effect on men who had stood up to far worse during the war.

Draper ordered Toronto's whole fleet of police motorcycles to surround the crowd, with their exhausts pointing inwards, toward the protesters. They began spewing dense clouds of blue smoke, reminiscent of the deadly gases in the trenches, but the veterans stood their ground and, after a while, Draper ordered a withdrawal.

Danny, relieved but still feeling guilty, turned his horse toward his station and stable on the other side of the city.

He was off duty the following two days and was glad of it when he read the morning paper on the second day. His unit was being criticized once again because they had only provided two mounted officers to protect a group of Jewish men from a band of Nazi fanatics in Christie Pits Park. Chief Draper was quoted as saying the Jews had been 'provocative by having their picnic and baseball game in such a well-used public place.'

Shades of Russia, Danny thought as he slammed the paper down.

He picked up and reread the letter from his lawyer in Middleton. It was bad news: Angie had passed away. As far as the lawyer could determine, she had succumbed to tuberculosis. The local doctor had recommended that she be sent to the sanatorium in

The Secret of the Spring

Kentville, but they had refused to take her, saying all their beds were full.

Full of English faces, Danny thought.

There was a copy of her death certificate included with the letter. It said she had died at Bear River. *At least she was with her family.*

Tommy was still in England, though, and tracking him down was increasingly difficult. Danny wondered if he would ever manage to pass the news along.

"I have it from the attending doctor," the lawyer had added, "that her last words included your name and something about a red tin. I cannot fathom their meaning. If, as per your previous instructions, to wit, after Angeline Arseneau's death, you wish your property and the contents thereof to be sold by auction and the proceeds sent to you, I shall arrange it immediately."

Danny had received a sizable bequest from his mother and father's estate as soon as he returned from the war—enough to buy the house in Parkdale, on the west side of Toronto. He had set aside funds for Aunt Angeline, who had looked after the house for him after his parents passed away and he was still overseas.

She'd sent him a few keepsakes, but for the most part, Danny liked to keep his memories in his mind. Angie had continued to live in the house until her recent move to Bear River and he frequently sent letters to the lawyer with instructions to forward them on to her.

With Lilly gone, Angie found it difficult to do the writing herself, so her news back to him was always terse. She often mentioned that there was something very important that she needed to tell him, but that she could not say it in a letter. It would have to wait until he came for a visit so she could tell him in person.

His wife, Margaret, was very understanding about what Danny had been doing for Angeline. She knew that Angeline had been a second mother to him and that he was bound to look after her. They were doing all right: thirteen years of marriage, three healthy children and a lovely home. Danny missed the country, but if he had to be in the city, his job with the horses was the closest substitute he could hope for.

What Margaret didn't understand was why, when they had been so close to his home when they disembarked in Halifax on their way home from Russia, he had refused to take her to the Valley for a visit and insisted that they carry on directly to Toronto. He had never explained completely, and there was something about the way he reacted when she pressed him that suggested that some things were best left alone.

53: Today, Mabel had been lucky

Middleton, Nova Scotia
June 1, 1934

Mabel Stronach loved auctions. She attended every one she could, sometimes driving her Model T Coupe as far as twenty miles when she saw a good one advertised.

She was a single woman. It wasn't by choice; in her youth there had been plenty of young men she would have been happy to marry, but she was a plain woman and no one had seemed to want her. She was tall and gangly and, at fifty years of age, she wore thick glasses and kept her graying hair in a tight bun on the back of her head. Early in life, in lieu of a suitable man, she had given her heart to Jesus and the local Baptist church became her solace. She devoted almost all of her free time to the various events on the church calendar.

Her only other real passion was following auctions. When she first started following up on the newspaper ads and posters, some of the more pious members of her congregation suggested that the practice was tawdry and unbecoming, but she was able to justify her habit by providing a continuous supply of items for the church bazaars and sales.

Nobody could argue with the extra money they provided for the upkeep of the parish.

In truth, though, not all the treasures she had accumulated made their way to the church. Mabel was a secret hoarder. She never entertained any of the other ladies at her home; in the early years she used her ailing mother as an excuse. Later, after her mother's death, people had become accustomed to her strange behaviour in this regard. Mabel was invited to other homes but nobody ever expected to see the inside of hers.

If they had, they would have been shocked. Over the years she had filled the rooms of the old house, box by box, leaving just enough room at the front of each room to give the impression of spaciousness should anyone come to the door.

She never bought big items at the auctions; she had no use for any more furniture. She liked the boxes that the auctioneer crammed full of the things he termed 'smalls': odd pieces of china, bottles of buttons, and the like. These boxes often contained personal items like post cards and letters, which gave Mabel a guilty thrill as she glimpsed into the lives of the people who had owned these tiny treasures.

She read whatever she found, but she wouldn't keep or pass on anything she deemed sensitive. Once she had been mortified by the discovery of a collection of pornographic postcards that a veteran had brought home from France. Looking at the big-breasted naked women lying in suggestive poses had

The Secret of the Spring

made her physically ill and she dropped them in disgust. Eyes almost closed, she dared to touch them just once more to tear them up and throw them in her kitchen stove.

That's when she decided that she would become a censor of sorts, making sure that nothing remotely like those postcards would ever see the light of day again. Any religious items that were not compatible with her Baptist beliefs met a similar fate.

Today Mabel had been lucky. The auction was just a couple of miles from her home in Middleton and the rumble seat of her little car was crammed with cardboard boxes filled with treasures.

Although she hadn't purchased any of the major items, she had been really surprised by the contents of the house as item after item came out the front door and fell under the auctioneer's gavel. There was the usual furniture and household effects, but among them were many things that seemed strangely out of place: all kinds of military paraphernalia, flashy uniforms, sabres, pistols and several colourful framed prints depicting famous cavalry engagements. One print showing a trooper of the 17th Lancers was particularly beautiful and brought a good price.

Everyone attending was astonished by the bizarre items and wondered how they had come into hands of the old French woman who'd occupied the property. Some unkind speculations were bandied about, but Mabel felt it more Christian to give the old woman the benefit of the doubt. Anyway, she was pleased with her purchases and looked forward to getting them home.

She had only one more stop to make. Her mother had once worked as a housekeeper at the old Spa Springs Hotel and had become a believer in the healing powers of the water. The hotel was long gone, but the spring still existed in a pine grove near where the hotel had been and it was on her way. She didn't believe that there was anything particularly special about the water, but old habits die hard and, even after her mother's death, Mabel continued to fill a jug of the water for herself now and again, just in case.

She stopped her little car and went around to the passenger side, opened the door and retrieved her water container. As she closed the door she noticed a bright red cake tin protruding from one of the boxes in the rumble seat. She had meant to have a look in the tin back at the auction but got in a hurry and hadn't bothered.

Thinking it might be amusing to have a look at its contents while she waited for her water can to fill, she took it out of the box and, with it in one hand and her container in the other, followed the path down to spring.

The remnants of the spring house were still there, and there was a rickety bridge that she had to carefully make her way over. The spring itself was cribbed in a square of rotting timber, but was constantly bubbling up and over the casement and cascading down over a series of big rocks until it joined

The Secret of the Spring

the brook that traversed the property. If she placed her container just so under one of these rocks she didn't need to dip the water herself—Mother Nature would do the work.

Once she was sure that the container was ready, steady and upright, she found a dry spot to sit down and turned her attention to the red tin. It didn't appear to have been opened for a long time and there was rust where the top met the base, making it difficult to open. She broke a fingernail in her first attempt and uttered a Baptist substitute for a curse, then tried again. This time the top popped off and the contents were exposed.

At first glance nothing special caught her eye—just an old letter on yellow scribbler paper and, beneath it, a heavy crude ring. It was gold in colour but surely was only brass, something won at a carnival.

Mabel picked the letter up and began to read. She quickly concluded that she had stumbled onto the mad ravings of some demented woman—certainly not fit for anyone else's eyes.

She put the letter down and picked up the ring. She could see the weird-looking animals inscribed on it and imagined it to be something that might have been used in a pagan ritual.

She knew what she had to do. She climbed back up to the spring and dropped the ring into the swirling water. It caught the light and it gleamed briefly as it spiralled down, disappearing into the depths. Mabel had heard that the spring was bottomless and she hoped it was true.

Garry Leeson

Returning to where she had left the letter, she said a brief prayer for the poor soul who had written it, then tore the pages over and over again and dropped them in the overflow of the spring.

At first the pieces stayed together, but as they flowed along in the brook they began to separate, spreading out as the current whirled and eddied. They made their way under the bridge, flickering in the light. By the time they floated past the site of the old hotel they had stretched out into a long flotilla of bits of paper with blurring ink.

The brook carried them further down through orchards and fields and past the town of Middleton. By the time the soggy fragments of the letter reached the Annapolis River, the words had faded and were gone forever.

The Secret of the Spring

Garry Leeson

On alternate historical fiction

Several real people appear as characters in these pages, and in some cases I have inserted my fictional characters into events that really happened.

The Spa Springs Hotel did exist and all the events surrounding Captain Hall that I describe are more or less substantiated in local lore and literature. It seems almost certain that the Prince of Wales spent some time at the hotel in 1889. The hotel register preserved at the Nova Scotia Public Archives does not have a record of the visit—strangely the page corresponding with the suggested time of his stay has been torn out. His relationship with my character, Lilly, is simply wild conjecture on my part but given the class distinctions and morals of the time, it would not have been that unusual.

All the events that occurred during the time that I have my character, Ben Johnson, spending with the 17th Lancers are real, and his descriptions, analysis and opinions reflect those of some of the great minds of the period like Rudyard Kipling. My description of the horrible events surrounding the murder of my Acadian character, Alphonse Arseneau, draws on an unsolved crime in the area. His story is not intended to be connected in any way with that of the real victim who met his terrible demise in a similar way, in a year less distant.

Alternate historical fiction is a popular and exciting sub-genre of speculative fiction. Alternate history novels craft a fictional narrative with a mixture of both true and imagined historical context to create a world that's both familiar and enjoyably different to readers.

If, by blending historical icons with the figments of my imagination, I have blurred the line between fact and fiction, then I have achieved what I set out to do.

GHLL

Acknowledgements

Of course without the amazing assistance of my editor, Andrew Wetmore, this book would not exist.

Without my two daughters, Zoe and Emily, I would never have continued this journey.

Artistic assistance from Rebekah Wetmore and Gabrielle Rail, and from first reader Pat Labor.

And as always, Andrea.

Garry Leeson

About the author

Garry Leeson is an award-winning author, playwright, auctioneer, and by times, logger and farmer, from the Annapolis Valley in Nova Scotia. His works have appeared in periodicals in Canada and USA; his plays have had productions in Kentville and Lunenburg and CBC Radio has showcased his short stories.

He was long-listed for CBC Writes in the Creative Nonfiction category in 2012. He was a recipient of an Arts Nova Scotia grant and in 2020 received the

Margaret and John Savage First Book Award for Non-Fiction for his book, *The Dome Chronicles*.

Garry continues to live with his wife, Andrea, and a menagerie of animals, in the community of Harmony.

For the curious of mind, visit garryleeson.com

Also by Garry Leeson

The Dome Chronicles
Nevermore Press

Winner: 2021 Margaret and John Savage First Book Award (Non-Fiction)

A humorous collection of true stories, centred around a back-to-the-land endeavour, and a unique building structure.

Leeson writes with astute observation of the absurdity of the best-laid plans with joyous self-deprecation.

His stories focus as much on the community

around him—the stoic and staid farm folk—as they do on his family's own foibles and successes. As he tries to eke out a sustainable existence, the locals teach him a way of life deeply rooted in community and heritage.

At the same time, he documents a continental movement, the 1970s back-to-the-landers, mighty in number and determined to find a better, more authentic, way to live.

The book is greatly enhanced by personal photographs in black and white, adding to the charming sense of tradition and sustainability. The last sentence of the collection leaves the book open, so to speak, to another chapter, perhaps a follow-up to this one's success.

—Atlantic Books Today, Awards East Review

Book club discussion guide

Here are some questions you can use as jumping-off points as you discuss *The Secret of the Spring.*

1. Given that literary fiction focuses on style and depth and is character-driven, and genre fiction is plot-driven, focusing on imaginary details, where would you place *The Secret of the Spring*? How would you describe the style of the book: an historical fiction, a literary fiction or even, perhaps, an historical romance?
2. How did you find the roles and descriptions of the various true-life characters in the book? Did they enhance the story for you, making it more believable?
3. How did you relate to the tough times Ben had lived through in his life? Was it possible for him to truly escape their influence or do you think he just suppressed them?
4. How would the plot have been affected if Lilly had told Ben what the Prince of Wales had done when she first went to live at the smithy?
5. Considering the age difference between Ben and Lilly, did you find their relationship was plausible? Do you know couples like them? How would things have been different if they were closer in age?

6. Does the omniscient narration style enhance the Victorian feel of the book?
7. Discuss the conditions of Lilly's early life and how it has or has not become a thing of the past, either here in Canada or elsewhere. Would there be help now for her? How would her situation have become known now and what could have been done for her and her family today?
8. When Victoria became Queen, she banned 'royal bastards' from Court, calling them "ghosts best forgotten." What options would Danny have had in today's world, if he knew his father may have been a member of the royal family? And how would Lilly's life have been different?
9. An early reader of the manuscript suggested that the story was essentially about the cruelty of men. How have things changed or remained the same since the era of this book (1880s-1930s)?
10. Lilly's letter never gets to Danny, so he continues to suspect the worst about his parentage. Is that a satisfactory ending?
11. Would you want to read the rest of the story in a sequel? Where do you think the story will go?

www.ingramcontent.com/pod-product-compliance
Lightning Source LLC
Chambersburg PA
CBHW071411070526
44578CB00003B/551